Strolling in Macau

A Visitor's Guide to Macau, Taipa, and Coloane

Strolling in Macau:
A Visitor's Guide to Macau, Taipa, and Coloane
By Steven K. Bailey
Photographs by Jill C. Witt

Cover and book design by Janet McKelpin/Dayspring Technologies, Inc.
Editing assistance provided by Chi-Ming Chien

Please be advised that restaurants, shops, businesses and other establishments in this book have been written about over a period of time. The editor and publisher have made every effort to ensure the accuracy of the information included in this book at the time of publication, but prices and conditions may have changed, and the editor, publisher and authors cannot assume and hereby disclaim liability for loss, damage or inconvenience caused by errors, omissions or changes in regard to information included in this book.

For information regarding permissions, write to:
ThingsAsian Press
3230 Scott Street
San Francisco, California 94123 USA
www.thingsasianpress.com
Printed in Singapore

ISBN-10: 0-9715940-9-0
ISBN-13: 978-0-9715940-9-8

TABLE OF CONTENTS

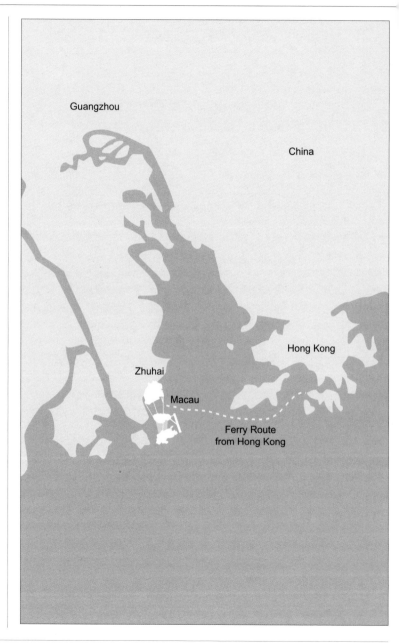

THE PEARL RIVER DELTA

Guangzhou

China

Hong Kong

Zhuhai

Macau

Ferry Route
from Hong Kong

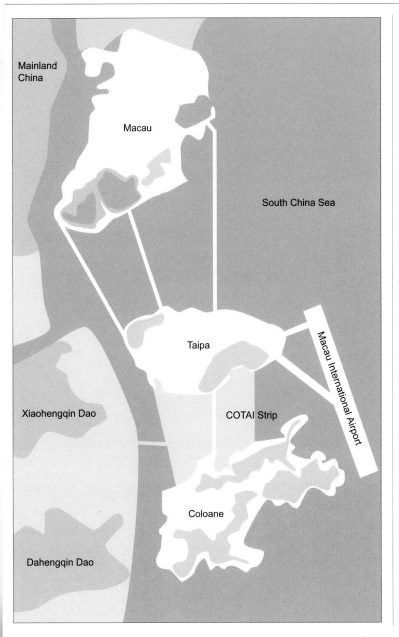

MACAU

Mainland China

Macau

South China Sea

Taipa

Macau International Airport

Xiaohengqin Dao

COTAI Strip

Coloane

Dahengqin Dao

Introduction

I once interviewed a senior administrator in the Macau Public Security Forces. At the time I was doing a freelance article on Macau for a CNN print magazine, though I had also written several pieces on Macau for the Asia travel website ThingsAsian. The administrator was familiar with these articles, and at one point during our conversation said that he had agreed to meet with me not so much because of my association with CNN, but because I was clearly, as he put it, "a friend of Macau." I took this as a great compliment, for I do indeed consider myself a friend of that unique city on the South China Sea. That friendship, in fact, is my primary motivation for writing this guidebook.

I hope to convince you to visit Macau, and once there, help you to experience all that makes Macau so fascinating. In other words, I want you to become a friend of Macau as well.

When writing this guidebook, I assumed that like most foreign visitors, you will be making a short trip to Macau—probably less than 24 hours, but certainly not more than a few days. For this reason, I have provided limited information about accommodations in Macau. The historic Pousada de Sao Tiago remains the notable exception to this rule, as you will find this unusual hotel to be worth a visit even if you are not staying there.

I have also assumed that you will be traveling to Macau aboard a ferry from Hong Kong. After all, while the Taiwanese fly to Macau and the mainland Chinese simply walk across the border, just about everybody else travels to Macau by ferry. This one-hour journey has become a quintessential part of any trip to Macau, in fact, and I never fail to enjoy it.

In addition, I have assumed that *unlike* most foreign tourists, you have not come to gamble and do not wish to lose your money in one of the city's many casinos. Consequently, while this guidebook does discuss the impact of legalized gambling on

Macau, it does not contain any practical information about the casinos themselves.

I have made no assumptions about your nationality; however, I have assumed that you speak neither Portuguese nor Cantonese. If you do happen to speak Cantonese—as some readers from Hong Kong will, for example—then the portions of this book dealing with the language barrier in Macau can obviously be disregarded.

Lastly, and perhaps most importantly, I have assumed that you want to walk. After all, Macau is best explored on foot and remains one of the most pedestrian-friendly cities in Asia.

Macau's walkability is just one of its many appealing features, which is why I believe the city deserves its own guidebook rather than a single chapter at the end of a guide to Hong Kong. Hong Kong guidebooks tend to repeat the same standard clichés about Macau, describing it as a seedy Monte Carlo of the Orient lost in the shadows of Hong Kong. Rarely do these guides provide more detailed insights into a city with a deeper and more nuanced history than Hong Kong. Though it may be much smaller than Hong Kong, Macau's complexities nonetheless demand more than a single chapter. They demand, in fact, an entire book.

Writing such a book comes with its share of challenges, including Macau's multilingual heritage. For example, a street in Macau can be known by up to four competing names—one each for English, Portuguese, Cantonese, and Mandarin. However, there is no consistency in usage; in English, for example, some Portuguese and Cantonese place names are generally translated while others are left in the original language (and in the case of Cantonese and Mandarin, there may be competing Romanized spellings of the place name to further confuse the issue).

In the interest of consistency and clarity, I have tried to use the version of place names most commonly used in English-language texts. Thus throughout this guidebook I refer to Avenida de Almeida Ribeiro by its Portuguese name, and not by its English translation of Almeida Ribeiro Avenue or its entirely different Cantonese name of San Ma Lo (or its English translation of New Street). Following the same rule, I refer to Senate Square by its English name, rather than the Portuguese Largo do Senado or the pidgin Senado Square.

I have tried to make this guidebook as historically accurate as possible. However, another challenge of writing about Macau is the often incomplete and/or contradictory nature of historical information. The further back into Macau's history you go, the more likely you will run into accounts that over the centuries have acquired the weight of fact, but in reality cannot be verified. Did a sharp-shooting Jesuit priest named Jeronimo Rho *really* fire the cannonball that destroyed the Dutch powder supply, thereby routing the invaders and saving Macau in 1622? Or is this an embellishment that might better be classified as historical legend? Well, it seems that nobody really knows. In cases such as these, I have inserted qualifying words or phrases into the text like "supposedly" or "according to legend." In all cases I have tried to verify facts from multiple sources. When information conflicted I have either accepted the most reliable source's ruling or noted the contradictory nature of that information.

Having said all this, I fully recognize that errors of fact or interpretation will inevitably appear in this guidebook. I take full responsibility for these mistakes, apologize for any inadvertent confusion they might cause, and thank you in advance for calling my attention to them. I should also warn that Macau is in the midst of a massive construction binge involving new roadways, light-rail lines, hotels, high-rises, golf courses, casinos, and even entire city districts reclaimed from the sea. The Pharaonic scale of this construction as well as the rapid pace of change in Macau means that some of the information contained in this book will inevitably be outdated by the time you make your journey to Macau. To correct errors or update information for future editions of this guidebook, please send me an email at *sbailey@thingsasian.com*.

More people helped me write this guidebook than I could possibly thank. However, I would like to express my gratitude to those people whose help I could not have done without. Albert Wen of ThingsAsian Press gave me free reign to develop this guidebook as I saw fit, but never wavered in his commitment to publish a guidebook truly worthy of Macau. I would like to thank my friends Nathan and Rachel Carpenter for going above and beyond the call of duty and taking in our dogs while Jill and I were in Asia researching this book. In Macau, I want to thank Antonieta Lourenco Lei and the staff of the Emperor Hotel. I also wish to thank Alorino Noruega and especially Teresa Costa Gomes, whose energy, enthusiasm, and multilingual knowledge of Macau made her the perfect guide. Most of all, I wish to thank my wife Jill Witt for the photographs accompanying the text of this book as well as for her unwavering support and faith in my ability to complete this project.

Steven K. Bailey

The iconic ruins of St. Paul's Cathedral take on a haunted beauty at night.

MACAU'S DUAL HERITAGE

For nearly five centuries, Macau has blended Portuguese and Cantonese culture into a unique mix found nowhere else in the world.

The First Portuguese Arrive

The first Portuguese sailors to reach Macau came by ship, just as you most likely will—galleon in their case, jetfoil in yours. I often wonder what those first Portuguese adventurers were thinking when the mysterious coast of China finally appeared on the horizon after their long voyage from Europe, round the Horn of Africa to India, and on through the straights of Malacca to the South China Sea. Perhaps they had already met Chinese mariners in the Portuguese colony at Malacca; at the very least they would have heard tales that portrayed China as a land of deadly peril and fantastic riches.

As they approached that mysterious and forbidding coast, those first Portuguese adventurers would have called on their skills as mariners, traders, soldiers, and diplomats even while simultaneously recognizing that only the grace of their Catholic god would keep them from harm. As for the reputed riches of China, these men had not come to pillage like the Spanish conquistadors in the Americas, though they were not above such rapacious actions. A more subtle form of avarice propelled these Portuguese eastward—a lust for trade with the legendary Far East, with its silk, spices, porcelain, jade, and other treasures.

Quite literally seeking his fortune, a Portuguese adventurer named Jorge Alvares first reached the shores of China in 1513. Other Portuguese galleons soon followed, and for the next 40 years they plied the waters of East Asia in armed merchant ships. After a series of abortive attempts to found a permanent base on the Chinese coast, a motley assortment of Portuguese sailors, priests, merchants, and military officers landed in the Bay of A-Ma, which the locals called A-Ma Gao and the Portuguese corrupted into the name "Macau."

In 1557, Macau officially became the first European settlement on the Chinese coast—a colony that four centuries later the poet

---

Lead photo description on page 191

W. H. Auden would describe as "a weed from Catholic Europe." Local Chinese mandarins and their distant Ming dynasty emperor saw no harm in letting the foreign barbarians set up a trading port in Macau, a tiny spit of worthless land and a few rocky islets of no use to the emperor. To fence in the Portuguese traders, the mandarins erected a barrier wall across the top of the peninsula. Despite establishing this de-facto border, however, the Chinese never recognized Lisbon's sovereignty over Macau and made it clear that the continued presence of the Portuguese depended on their tributary payments and the blessing of the emperor.

From the very beginning, the mandarins and emperor alike viewed the nascent colony of Macau as a door to the outside world that could, if necessary, be slammed shut to keep the foreign barbarians at bay. The Chinese calculated that their uncouth but useful guests could facilitate trade with Europe and other regions of Asia, but be easily ejected if they became troublesome.

The foreign barbarians had their feet firmly inside the door, however, and through manipulation and negotiation, bribery and canny marketeering, managed to make Macau a permanent guest in the Chinese house. The Portuguese never held Macau by force; in fact, they never had the military muscle in Asia to get what they wanted through force of arms. Like all Portuguese settlements in Asia, Macau remained highly vulnerable. While the colony's extensive fortifications ensured it could ward off small-scale raids by local pirates or rival colonial powers, ultimately the city was indefensibly small and never garrisoned with enough troops to resist a determined attack from the Chinese mainland. Understanding this reality, the Portuguese continued to make themselves useful to the right people in China and, in the process, enriched themselves and those they did business with.

Portugal was vying with Spain to become the world's dominant maritime power. While it lacked the strength to colonize Asia by force, it did have sufficient ships, crews, and captains to maintain a far-flung and often tenuous trading network connecting China and Japan with India, Africa, Brazil, and Europe. Macau became a key link in a chain of Portuguese ports that stretched across the globe. After stopping at the Portuguese colonies of Goa and Malacca—on the coasts of present-day India and Malaysia, respectively—Portuguese ships would continue north to Macau. At that time China had banned its subjects from trading with Japan directly, leaving the Portuguese ideally poised to function as middlemen. After taking on a load of Chinese silk, their ships would continue on to the Portuguese enclave in Nagasaki, Japan. There they would swap the silk and other goods for silver, which they then sold to Chinese buyers in Macau for a huge profit in gold. Loaded with this gold—or the goods bought with it—some ships then retraced their route back to Lisbon. However, much of the wealth generated by the China-Japan trade stayed in Macau.

Though founded by Portuguese traders as a business venture, Macau also became command central for the Jesuits, missionaries, and other assorted Catholic zealots seeking to spread their religion across Asia. In 1586, Macau's growing importance as a center for trade as well as Catholic proselytizing led the Portuguese crown to officially recognize the colony with the title *Cidade do Nome de Deus*—The City of the Name of God. Not surprisingly, the colony's first European buildings included several Catholic churches, most famously St. Paul's, erected by the Jesuits in 1602.

Several local temples predated St. Paul's, however. At the head of the Macau peninsula, Chinese fishermen had long worshipped at the A-Ma Temple, dedicated to a patron deity of the same name. The Jesuits' flexible version of Catholicism and the equally elastic religious practices of the locals soon began to overlap, so much so that at times converted Chinese Catholic residents observed elements of Catholicism, Taoism, and Buddhism simultaneously and without any apparent contradiction. This blending of European and Asian religions remains emblematic of the cross-cultural fusion that characterized Macau from its very inception.

The Macanese occupied the center of this cross-cultural fusion. Members of this tight-knit community were part Portuguese and part Cantonese, with traces of other colonial bloodlines as well—Japanese, Angolan, Brazilian, Goan, Malay. Though they invariably spoke both Portuguese and Cantonese, they also spoke Patua, a dialect based on Portuguese but influenced by Cantonese and other tongues. The Macanese practiced Catholicism as well as traditional Chinese practices such as ancestor worship and *feng shui*. Their eclectic cuisine borrowed ingredients and recipes from not just southern China and Portugal, but the entire Portuguese colonial empire as well. Able to move among the colonial Portuguese as well as among the local Cantonese, the Macanese wielded considerable influence in a colony that enjoyed a century-long period of wealth and prosperity based largely on its key role in the silk trade with Japan.

The End of the Golden Age

From about 1560 to 1639, Macau remained the hub of the lucrative silk and silver trade between China and Japan. This attracted the attention of the Dutch, who like the Portuguese had sailed East for commerce rather than conquest. They sought to supplant the Portuguese as door wardens to the China trade and used their conflict in Europe against the Spanish—who from 1580 to 1640 occupied Portugal—as justification for attacking Macau.

On June 24, 1622, a Dutch fleet under Captain Kornelis Reyerszoon assembled a landing force of some 800 armed sailors, a number thought more than sufficient to overpower Macau's relatively weak garrison. Macau's future as a Dutch colony seemed all but assured, since the city's fortifications still remained under construction and its defenders numbered only about 60 soldiers and 90 civilians, who ranged from Jesuit priests to African slaves.

The Dutch invaders bombarded the city and then came ashore at Cacilhas Beach—now the site of the present-day city reservoir. As the Dutch advanced on the city, the defenders called for the protection of Sao Tiago (St. James), the patron saint of Portuguese soldiers, and commenced firing. According to legend, a Portuguese priest named Jeronimo Rho, who had a predilection for the military arts, fired a cannonball that hit the Dutch gunpowder supply. Accounts differ on whether Father Rho scored a direct hit on an ammunition wagon or the magazine of a Dutch ship, but all agree that a spectacular explosion resulted. Seeing the massive blast and the damage it had caused, the outnumbered Portuguese charged the disorganized Dutch force, which fled in disarray. The Dutch left behind 136 casualties and thus ended Holland's ambitions to control Macau.

Though Father Rho and his multi-talented Jesuits had saved Macau, they ultimately contributed to its decline as well. By converting some 150,000 Japanese Catholics, who threatened the status quo with their foreign beliefs, the Jesuits earned the ire of the Japanese authorities. As a result, in 1639 the Japanese expelled the Portuguese from their trading port in Nagasaki, the source of much of Macau's wealth. The silk trade that had enriched Macau ended, and the city's golden age drew to a close to the anguished cries of martyred Japanese Catholics.

Meanwhile, the Dutch had their revenge for their defeat at Macau. In 1641, they took the Portuguese port of Malacca after an eight-month siege. Malacca had served as a key way station for Portuguese ships sailing to Macau, and its loss just two years after the expulsion from Nagasaki left Macau isolated and increasingly irrelevant to Lisbon. Macau's misfortunes coincided with a more general decline in the Portuguese colonial empire, further ensuring the tiny enclave's slide into relative obscurity.

The indefatigable Jesuits, however, continued their efforts to Catholicize China. Though the Jesuits never succeeded in converting many Chinese, the Chinese did succeed in converting the Jesuits, who learned the language, wore local dress, and mastered the fine art of calligraphy. The Jesuits did not renounce their Catholicism, but they did reconcile it with traditional Chinese practices such as ancestor worship. Led by priests like the Italian Matteo Ricci, the Jesuits fostered an enlightened cultural exchange that lasted nearly a century, with Macau representing Europe. Ricci and his comrades dazzled the imperial court with clocks, celestial globes, telescopes, and other Western technology. In turn, the Jesuits studied every aspect of the Chinese empire, which they greatly admired.

The Jesuit efforts in China faltered when the Vatican ruled against the Jesuit belief that newly converted Catholics could continue to practice ancestor worship and other central tenets of Chinese culture. In the Jesuit view, these were secular rites compatible with the Christian faith—a position that led to the long-running Rites Controversy, in which the papacy decisively ruled against the Jesuits. Further doctrinal disputes and power struggles within the Catholic Church led to the expulsion of the Jesuits from Macau in 1762. The remarkable cross-cultural dialogue fostered by the Jesuits ended with their departure from the colony, and the characteristics of that enlightened conversation—education and learning, respect and tolerance—would be distinctly absent from later colonial encounters.

These colonial encounters involved European and American merchants seeking quick profits in the China trade. Beginning in the 1770s, the mandarins allowed foreign merchants to trade in nearby Canton (Guangzhou), an arrangement that reduced Macau's importance as a doorway to China. However, the mandarins restricted this trade to an annual period running from October to May. In addition, no foreign men could reside in Canton during the summer months; foreign women remained banned from Canton year round. This imperial decree benefited Macau, as the Western merchants had no choice but to maintain homes in the Portuguese colony, many of them elaborate villas and mansions along the Praia Grande. The British East India Company operated out of Macau at this time, renting a mansion near the site of the present-day Camoes Garden. While this period hardly generated the fantastic riches that had poured into Macau during the days of the silk trade with Japan, enough wealth flowed through the colony to keep it relatively prosperous.

The rising power of Great Britain changed Macau's fortunes irrevocably, however. The British, who had surpassed the Portuguese, Dutch, and Spanish to become the world's dominant colonial power, wanted to trade with China, but could find little the Chinese wanted to buy except opium. British ships picked up loads of opium in India, hauled it to China, and traded the addictive narcotic primarily for tea, but also for silk, porcelain, and other goods. Southern Chinese merchants profited alongside the British traders, as did Macanese middlemen and freelancing American clipper captains with cargoes of opium from Turkey.

The Ching imperial court, represented in Canton by the morally upright mandarin Lin Zexu, eventually took exception to British drug dealing. In 1839, Lin Zexu destroyed 20,000 confiscated chests of English opium. At this point the British departed Canton for Macau or the protected anchorage of Hong Kong Island. Later that year Lin Zexu demanded that all British citizens be banned from Macau—an edict the Portuguese governor obeyed. Some 250 British subjects—including the landscape painter George Chinnery, still to this day the colony's most famous British resident—fled Macau for Royal Navy warships and British-flagged merchant vessels anchored off of Taipa Island. Rather than meekly sail for home, however, the British chose to stand and fight over the opium trade. This led to a peculiar conflict sparked by the Chinese emperor's refusal to let British merchants peddle opium in China.

THE RISE OF HONG KONG

In 1842, after the brief Sino-British conflict known as the Opium War, the British acquired Hong Kong Island from China. The unequal treaty ending the short-lived war granted Hong Kong, situated some 40 miles (65 km) northeast of Macau across the Pearl River Delta, to the British in perpetuity. This made Hong Kong, for all practical purposes, part of Britain—and the British Royal Navy had the military muscle to ensure it remained that way. For these reasons, Hong Kong remained profoundly different from Macau, which had never been transferred to Portuguese sovereignty—and even if it had been, could not have been defended from any Chinese attempt to retake it.

With its fine deep-water port, Hong Kong soon replaced Macau as the wide-open door through which the outside world traded with southern China. Meanwhile, trade with northern China went through Shanghai, one of five "treaty ports" opened after the Opium War. Reflecting Hong Kong's growing importance as well as Britain's military superiority over China, in 1860 the colony expanded in size with the acquisition in perpetuity of the Kowloon Peninsula, and later the adjacent New Territories on a 100-year lease. This made Hong Kong much larger than Macau in terms of both population and landmass.

Macau also expanded in size at this time, though on a far smaller scale than Hong Kong. The colonial governor of Macau took control of three small islands off the southern tip of the colony in 1847 and then took over the much larger Coloane Island in 1864—a land grab facilitated by the power of other colonial nations such as Great Britain, which had forced China to accept humiliations like the cession of Hong Kong and the opening of the treaty ports. If Britain, France, and other Western countries had not already forced China to accept their demands, it is unlikely that Macau could have unilaterally expanded its borders or convinced Chinese authorities to sign, in 1887, a treaty granting Portugal the right to administer Macau indefinitely.

Despite the 1887 treaty and Macau's increased size, the colony's fortunes steadily declined from the mid-1800s until the Second World War. Macau became a somnolent colonial backwater, its silted-up harbor too shallow for the deeper drafts of steamships, and its grand old colonial buildings sadly neglected. For a few decades Macau cashed in on the exploitative coolie trade, shipping laborers off to far-flung places like Cuba, Peru, Hawaii, Sumatra, and Malaya for indentured servitude. At this time the governor also legalized casino gambling—a fateful decision that would profoundly shape the colony's future. Smuggling prospered, along with assorted other vices like opium smoking and prostitution, and the colony acquired a reputation for the dissolute and the debauched, where an anything-goes mentality took hold that persists in somewhat watered-down form to the present day.

Despite Macau's declining fortunes, its population steadily increased as refugees from political chaos, famine, and conflict in China sought a safe haven—the most famous of these refugees being Dr. Sun Yat-Sen, founder of the Chinese Republic in 1911.

Whatever the limitations of Portugal's colonial rule, the country's neutral status during the Second World War saved Macau from the horrors of Japanese occupation. While Hong Kong and southern China fell to the Rising Sun, Macau remained a tiny island of calm protected by nothing more than the neutral status of an unimportant European country on the other side of the world. But the war years were hardly easy for Macau. The colony faced a severe food shortage while struggling to absorb an influx of refugees from southern China and Hong Kong. Refugees had to be housed in historic buildings like the Dom Pedro V Theatre and Bela Vista Hotel. Meanwhile, the Portuguese military resorted to selling its only gunboat, the *Macau*, to the Japanese; they also sold the historic antique cannons of Barra Fort (now the Pousada de Sao Tiago hotel) to scrap-metal dealers. The profits from these exchanges went to buy rice for the refugees. Overall, however, Macau fared well compared to Hong Kong, which endured four years of brutal Japanese occupation costing thousands of lives. Of all the European and American colonies in Asia, only Macau had escaped Japanese occupation and the devastation that followed.

Despite the wartime damage to Hong Kong, the British colony became a post-war economic dynamo that completely eclipsed Macau. A symbiotic relationship developed between the two colonies as Macau's smaller and weaker economy grew increasingly dependent upon Hong Kong dollars. British-run Hong Kong had plenty of cash, but no wish to soil its streets with gambling casinos; Portuguese-administered Macau had little money but no moral qualms about casinos and all the associated vices that went with them. Casino gambling soon became Macau's primary source of income, attracting high and low-rollers alike from the increasingly prosperous Hong Kong, but leaving the Portuguese enclave with a tawdry reputation for sleaze and corruption.

THE HANDOVER

In 1966, China's violent Cultural Revolution spilled over into Macau like some kind of red tsunami. Riots and other mayhem instigated by Chairman Mao's Red Guards made the city virtually ungovernable. As a result, Portugal threatened to hand the enclave back to China. The mainland government, recognizing Macau's valuable role as a trade conduit to the outside world, reined in the Red Guards and told the Portuguese to carry on.

In the 1970s, after the overthrow of the right-wing Salazar dictatorship in Lisbon, Portugal began to shed the last vestiges of its colonial empire. All around the world Portuguese colonies declared independence. In Asia only East Timor and tiny Macau remained of Portugal's colonial empire. But whereas East Timor declared independence in 1975, Macau remained a stubborn barnacle on the keel of China that not even the newly democratic Portuguese government could pry loose. In 1974 Lisbon once again offered to return Macau to China, which was in the final years of the politically chaotic Cultural Revolution and in no position to accept the offer even if it had wanted to. Beijing saw no need to change the status quo, since Macau still served as a useful gateway to the world economy, but more importantly, the mainland government wished to negotiate Hong Kong's return to China before dealing with the return of the much less important Macau. Despite China's refusal, the Portuguese government accepted that Macau would be Chinese by the end of the century, and in response to Chinese demands, officially recognized China's sovereignty over Macau and began to reduce its presence in the colony. In a highly symbolic move, the Portuguese military departed in 1975 after more than 400 years in Macau.

While the Portuguese did not dispute the Chinese claim to sovereignty over Macau, the British remained far less willing to return Hong Kong to China. From the standpoint of international law, they had no obligation to return Hong Kong Island and Kowloon, which had been ceded to them in perpetuity. From a practical standpoint, they had no choice, given that their 100-year lease on the New Territories would expire in 1997. Britain recognized that Hong Kong could not be broken up into separate pieces, with some continuing as colonial possessions and some returning to Chinese control, so in the 1980s Beijing and London began negotiating the terms of Hong Kong's return to China. Meanwhile, parallel negotiations went on between Beijing and Lisbon.

In what many observers saw as a fitting end to Great Britain's rule of Hong Kong, the negotiations over its handover were as unequal as the original negotiations in 1842 that had resulted in the British acquisition of the colony. This time China controlled the negotiating table, and though Beijing agreed to grant both Hong Kong and Macau a considerable degree of autonomy under the much-publicized "one country, two systems" formula, all parties understood that ultimately both colonies would be absorbed back into China on China's terms.

Hong Kong reverted to Chinese rule on the night of June 30, 1997, in a rain-soaked handover ceremony watched around the world. Nearly three years later, Macau's handover to China took place on December 20, 1999. As the roulette wheels kept spinning in nearby casinos, the colonial flag slid down the flagpole to be replaced by the red flag of China. The low-key event went largely unnoticed, though in some ways Macau's return was more historically significant than Hong Kong's. After all, when

President Jorge Sampaio returned Macau to China after 442 years of Portuguese rule, he closed the book on European colonialism in Asia. The Portuguese had been the first in and, despite their nation's fade from the world stage, the last out.

As it did with Hong Kong, the Chinese government designated Macau a Special Administrative Region (SAR). This meant the Macau SAR would remain an integral part of China but, in theory, enjoy considerable autonomy in all but foreign affairs and defense. Beijing pledged to let Macau run its own affairs for 50 years, but had already wavered on keeping a similar promise to neighboring Hong Kong. Macau's future remained clouded as a result, though most residents hoped that China would bring a newfound prosperity to the city after the economic doldrums of Portuguese rule and the Asian economic crisis of 1997. They also hoped that China would bring a semblance of order to the city, which had been suffering from gang violence related to its multibillion dollar gaming industry.

THE CASINOS

When the Portuguese colonial administration left for Lisbon, China inherited a city that had long been known as the Monte Carlo of the Orient. Media reports habitually referred to "the gambling enclave of Macau," and while this description unfairly reduced the city to a collection of slot machines, the fact remained that Macau's glitzy neon casinos generated several billion U.S. dollars per year, underpinned the economy, and contributed over 50 percent of the city's budget. The industry also supported numerous triad gangs, which thrived on loan sharking, illicit gambling, protection rackets, extortion, prostitution, and an assortment of other unsavory activities related to the casinos.

In the final years of Portuguese rule a particularly vicious spate of gang violence erupted between competing triads from Macau, China, Taiwan, and Hong Kong. Bloody gangland slayings left dozens of people dead, including several civil servants, and finally triggered a Portuguese crackdown. As a result, the police became targets themselves. In 1998, Macau's Judiciary Police chief Antonio Marques Baptista (a.k.a. Mr. Rambo) narrowly escaped being killed by a car bomb. Later that day he personally arrested notorious 14K Triad kingpin Wan Kwok-koi (a.k.a. Broken Tooth Koi) at the Lisboa Casino. Broken Tooth had chronicled his own violent career in the self-financed movie *Casino*, which was about to premiere in Hong Kong, but any sequel would have to be a prison film. After a local judge resigned, probably out of fear of a car bomb or other nasty surprise, a special judge flew in from Lisbon and sentenced Broken Tooth to 15 years in Macau prison on Coloane Island, though no clear connection to the car bomb was ever established. Various other associates of Broken Tooth went to prison as well, and three of his men nabbed in mainland China received a no-nonsense death sentence—a clear signal that Beijing backed the Portuguese efforts to curb the triads.

Despite the high-profile arrest and conviction of Broken Tooth, gang violence continued. Confidence in the city police, widely viewed as corrupt, plummeted. Media stories about the mayhem in Macau, a city normally absent from news headlines, appeared in newspapers worldwide. One respected Asian news magazine even compared Macau to Chicago in the days of Al Capone.

Though local government officials repeatedly claimed that the streets were safe, various governments cautioned their citizens not to visit the city. The U.S. State Department issued a travel advisory warning that while tourists were not the target of gang violence, they could potentially be caught in the crossfire. Already battered by the 1997 Asian economic crisis, the city's hotels, restaurants, and casinos suffered a further loss of revenue as nervous tourists gave Macau a miss. As a result, locals welcomed the handover not just because it meant the end of colonial rule, but because they wanted the incoming garrison of People's Liberation Army (PLA) troops to crush the triad gangs once and for all. Whereas the people of Hong Kong, many of whom hoped for democratic self rule, had greeted PLA troops with ambivalence, the more politically apathetic residents of Macau welcomed them as a rescuing force.

Violent crime did decline significantly after the handover. One police official told me that this decline stemmed from improved coordination between the Macau police and its counterparts in mainland China and Hong Kong. Other reports suggested that Macau's willingness to extradite gang members to China, with its fondness for the death sentence, helped bring the triads to heel. Regardless of the cause, the street violence ebbed and eventually the United States and other nations rescinded their travel advisories. Everyone understood, however, that as long as gambling continued to generate several billion dollars each year—not to mention over half of the city's revenue—then organized crime would continue to be as much a feature of the city as cobblestone streets and colonial architecture.

That said, I have always felt completely at ease in Macau, whether hiking secluded trails or walking narrow backstreets after nightfall. From the visitor's perspective, Macau remains a peaceful, orderly, and friendly place to visit. Street crime remains rare, and Macau certainly feels safer than many American or European cities of comparable size. As long as you don't try to horn in on triad business, your visit to Macau should be as safe as it is pleasant.

CULTURAL CROSSROADS

Many tourists—the vast majority of them from Hong Kong, mainland China, and Taiwan—come to Macau for the slot machines, *fan tan*, and baccarat. A growing number, however, come to experience the city's five-century fusion of Portuguese and Cantonese culture. They come to stroll Macau's southern European-style city center, with its narrow cobblestone streets, graceful tiled squares, and restored colonial buildings. They come to sample the city's gastronomic heritage as well, which blends Portuguese, African, Brazilian, and Chinese elements into a cuisine found nowhere else in the world.

The people of Macau take great pride in their historic city, and have made a concerted effort to preserve it. Unlike nearby Hong Kong, which has torn down most of its historic landmarks and replaced them with high-rise buildings, Macau has carefully maintained and restored its architectural heritage. Unlike so many other Asian metropolises, which have suffered the destruction of war and natural disaster, Macau has never been ravaged by fire, flood, or earthquake. Consequently the city boasts a wealth of historic churches, temples, villas, shophouses, and government edifices. These buildings can be found throughout the territory, though the majority lie in *centro da cidade*—the attractive city center with its half-Portuguese, half-Cantonese architecture.

Though dwindling, the Macanese community remains the living embodiment of Macau's dual Portuguese and Cantonese heritage. Following the Second World War so many Macanese emigrated that most people of such descent now live abroad. Fewer than one or two percent of Macau's population is now thought to be Macanese, though the very nature of the Macanese, who can blend so easily into the Chinese or Portuguese communities, makes them hard to count. Very few of the remaining Macanese speak the Patua dialect, though many continue to speak Portuguese. Despite their limited numbers, however, the Macanese continue to wield considerable influence. Because foreign passport holders can hold upper-level government positions in Macau—which is not true in Hong Kong—the many Macanese holding Portuguese passports have continued to serve as senior civil servants and government leaders. The Macanese are also involved in business, though this is an area traditionally dominated by the Cantonese.

The Cantonese, in fact, have always made up the vast majority of Macau's population. Today they account for 95% of Macau's estimated 465,000 inhabitants, making Macau a profoundly Cantonese metropolis. In fact, the same Cantonese business acumen that built Hong Kong also built up Macau's casinos into a multibillion dollar industry. The Cantonese influence can also be seen in the city's architecture, cuisine, and religious preferences—far more residents worship the goddess Kun Iam than the Virgin Mary. Cantonese remains the most common language by far, Chinese New Year trumps the Western version of the holiday, and the principles of *feng shui* determine the location and design of new buildings.

The already dominant Cantonese influence will only grow stronger as Macau's Macanese and expatriate Portuguese community continues to shrink. While the predicted post-handover exodus of Portuguese passport holders did not occur, a significant number of Portuguese citizens have nonetheless left the city. Pinning down the precise number of Portuguese nationals still living in Macau is tricky, because many are ethnic Chinese who also hold Macau SAR citizenship. Government sources claim that two percent of the population—about 10,000 people—is Portuguese. However, these same sources also claim that less than one percent of the population speaks Portuguese, which suggests that many of the Portuguese citizens living in Macau are really local Cantonese who thought it prudent to pick up a Portuguese passport just in case things soured after the handover.

Evidence of the decline in Portuguese influence can be found in everything from religion to air travel. Estimates on the number of Catholics range from five to fifteen percent of the total population, but regardless of the precise number, Catholicism clearly remains a minority faith in contemporary Macau. As further proof of the loosening ties between the city and its former colonial master, TAP Portugal no longer flies between Macau and Lisbon. How this reduced Portuguese presence will impact the character of the city remains to be seen, but it seems unlikely that nearly 500 years of Portuguese influence will disappear any time soon.

This is partially because Macau residents want to preserve their city's Portuguese flavor. This is a contradiction, of course, since like the people of Brazil, Angola, Mozambique, East Timor, and other Portuguese colonies, the residents of Macau were generally glad to see the Portuguese go. But even while repudiating their colonial rulers, they clearly intended to hold on to much that had resulted from those many centuries of Portuguese rule, be it the chilled white wine, the European Union passports, or the casinos—especially the casinos.

BUILDING FOR THE FUTURE

When I returned to Macau six months after the handover, I was struck not by how much had changed, but by how little. Barring a few minor details, in fact, post-handover Macau looked and felt no different than it did in the final years of Portuguese colonial rule. The green and white lotus-flower flag of Macau now flew over government buildings rather than the Portuguese standard, but the timeworn statues of Portuguese heroes like Vasco da Gama still stood throughout the city. A small contingent of PLA soldiers maintained a garrison beneath the Guia Hill lighthouse, one of the city's most famous landmarks, but they stayed off the streets and left policing the triads to the same local cops who had always had this unenviable task. Many of the city's powerbrokers still spoke Portuguese, and government ministries continued to churn out documents in both Portuguese and Cantonese. Basically, Macau appeared much the same on first glance—still slightly seedy and somewhat rundown, but also laidback, appreciative of the good things in life, and graced with an old-world charm.

While the handover had resulted in significant political change, economic change did not truly arrive until 2001 with the expiry of the 40-year monopoly gambling franchise held by the euphemistically named Macau Tourism and Amusement Company—better known by its Portuguese acronym of STDM. Billionaire Stanley Ho served as STDM's managing director and held a major stake in the corporation, which had interests in everything from casinos to construction. STDM even owned the ferries that hauled millions of cash-laden gamblers each year from Hong Kong. Though Stanley Ho was often described as the sole owner of the entire STDM empire, in fact a complex and at times shadowy mix of corporate and individual shareholders controlled its various components.

Though STDM and the high-profile Stanley Ho insisted they should retain the gambling monopoly, the government opted to open the gaming industry up to other players. Foreign investors and casino operators, many with interests in Las Vegas, began scrambling for a piece of the action in Macau—the only city with legalized casino gaming in China, a nation of 1.3 billion people. After renewing Stanley Ho's gambling concession, the government issued two more concessions to Hong Kong's Galaxy Entertainment and the Las Vegas-based Wynn Resorts.

As investors wagered heavily on the success of multimillion dollar casino deals, an army of construction cranes and an armada of land-reclamation barges besieged the city. Like some kind of gigantic magic trick, Macau's total landmass increased as more and more artificial land rose from the sea for flashy new casinos. Wynn Resorts broke ground on a massive hotel-casino located near the STDM-owned Lisboa Hotel, which had begun an ambitious expansion of its own. Operating under a sub-concession from Galaxy, the American-owned Las Vegas Sands opened the new Sands Macau, the city's largest casino, on the Macau peninsula.

Meanwhile, Las Vegas Sands began constructing an even larger complex of luxury casino-hotels in the COTAI district, the mile-long (1.6 km) strip of reclaimed land that joins Taipa and Coloane islands. The Sands dubbed its development the COTAI Strip, in honor of the famed Las Vegas Strip. The Venetian—modeled on the hotel-casino of the same name in Las Vegas—will serve as the centerpiece of this purpose-built gambling city. Scheduled to open in 2007, the Venetian will feature a mock indoor version of Venice, complete with gondolas and serenading gondoliers—and a simulated sky that changes from night to day and back again. Ironically, this means that as construction crews erect the Venetian they will have to build artificial canals on land that had itself been reclaimed from the sea. After all, gamblers on the COTAI Strip will be spinning roulette wheels on what used to be open water full of anchored China clippers, sampans, and junks.

Stanley Ho and his son Lawrence, still the dominant players in Macau, announced plans to build a casino on the COTAI Strip as well. In a not atypical Macau arrangement, some 450 gaming tables and 3,000 slot machines will jam the aptly named City of Dreams complex, which like most of the new casinos, reflected a Las Vegas approach to gaming in which the casino itself was a multifaceted entertainment complex.

The gambles taken by Stanley Ho's STDM and rival foreign casino operators look likely to pay off. After all, nearly 19 million foreigners visited Macau in 2005, the vast majority of them on gambling junkets. Punters from the mainland, Hong Kong, and Taiwan continue to pour into Macau like slot-machine tokens into a jackpot bucket. The city's 19 casinos—all but three owned by STDM—took in an astonishing 1.6 billion dollars in the first quarter of 2006 alone, resulting in tax revenues that easily funded more than half of the Macau government's budget.

The accelerating flow of gambling tax revenues has allowed Macau to embark on a series of massive public works projects—a third Macau-Taipa Bridge, a light-rail system, five new land-reclamation sites, and a container terminal, among others. Critics suggest that many of these projects will never pay for themselves, but will certainly enrich various corporations involved in their construction. They also suggest that these projects are designed to increase the government's popularity by pumping up the economy while simultaneously lowering the unemployment rate. All this would be fine with most residents, who hope that the gaming industry will continue to fuel the city's economy after years of painful economic recession.

While big casino complexes and other massive construction projects tend to attract the most attention, Macau has also invested heavily in the restoration of colonial buildings and other projects that preserve the city's cultural heritage. Unlike Hong Kong, which has pulled down virtually all of its historic buildings, Macau has proudly preserved its past. The casinos and other mega-projects have encased the older areas of Macau in a circle of reclaimed land, but they haven't destroyed them. The winding cobblestone streets, tiled plazas, and historic buildings of the Macau peninsula became a UNESCO World Heritage site in 2005. Macau's heritage has been successfully safeguarded, though the character of the city will undoubtedly change as it becomes more wealthy, more international, and more fast-paced.

I sometimes think that given the speed at which Hong Kong and Macau reclaim waterfront land, they will eventually fill in the entire Pearl River Delta and become one giant megalopolis.

This is not as farfetched as it sounds, as construction will soon begin on an 18-mile (29 km) super bridge linking Hong Kong and Macau. Soon you will be able to drive to Macau in half the time it now takes aboard a ferry. Visitors will no longer catch their first glimpse of Macau from the deck of a ship like those pioneering Portuguese sailors five centuries ago, but from the seat of a bus instead. The influence of those Portuguese sailors and all their compatriots who followed, however, will still remain. Macau's unique cross-cultural stew will continue to bubble, enriched by new arrivals like the city's vibrant Burmese community as well as entrepreneurs from Las Vegas and, of course, the mainland Chinese. Macau will remain an enchanting, if ever evolving, fusion of East and West. Like a good Portuguese wine, it can only get better with age.

❖ ❖ ❖

History at a Glance
Macau's history can be broken down into five distinct periods.

The Golden Age (1557–1639)
Portuguese merchants settle in Macau and grow fantastically rich from the silk and silver trade between China and Japan.

The Jesuits (1640–1762)
Based in Macau, the Catholic Jesuits lead an enlightened cultural exchange between Europe and China.

The Merchants (1762–1842)
European and American merchants use Macau as a base for trade with China.

The Rise of Hong Kong (1842–1945)
Hong Kong eclipses Macau as the doorway to China, causing the Portuguese colony to sink into dissolute decline.

The Casinos (1945 to present)
Macau becomes a modern city reliant on the revenue generated by its legalized casino gambling.

Air Raid Macau!

In 1945, neutral Macau found itself in the bombsights of planes launched from the American aircraft carrier USS Enterprise.

Anyone touring Macau's historic sites quickly learns of the abortive Dutch invasion of the city in 1622. Accounts of this failed assault invariably describe it as the only attack on Macau in its 500-year history. However, in an episode that all parties involved would just as soon forget, American naval aircraft repeatedly bombed Macau during the Second World War. Thus the United States and the Netherlands share the dubious honor of being the only countries to ever attack Macau.

Portugal declared itself a neutral power during World War II, which kept Macau free of Japanese occupation. Macau's population grew dramatically as a result, with war refugees streaming into the neutral haven from southern China. Most of the refugees were Chinese, but they also included Europeans fleeing the brutal Japanese occupation of Hong Kong.

The colonial administration under governor Gabriel Mauricio Teixeira struggled to house and feed thousands of refugees, who often arrived with just the clothes on their backs. Eventually Teixeira resorted to selling his meager military assets for cash to buy rice.

The colonial administration flogged its old cannons to scrap dealers; it also sold modern artillery parts from the Guia Hill fort and the colony's only gunboat to the Japanese. (Some accounts claim the Japanese unilaterally seized the gunboat after Portugal granted landing rights to American military aircraft in the Azores; if true, this would make the American bombing of Macau even more ironic.)

In early 1945, Governor Teixeira's administration offered to sell its stock of aviation gasoline to the Japanese military, which had run critically short of fuel. Stored at the Naval Aviation Center hangar on the Outer Harbor, the fuel had originally been earmarked for the colony's squadron of naval seaplanes, which by 1945 were no longer flying.

Local espionage agents immediately alerted the Americans of the impending avgas sale. The U.S. Navy resolved to destroy the stock of Portuguese fuel before it could be sold, as it feared the Japanese would use it to fill the tanks of the kamikaze planes that had been sinking American ships with such heavy loss of life.

On January 16, 1945, planes from the aircraft carrier USS *Enterprise* swooped down on Macau, blasting the naval seaplane hangar and fuel depot with 500-pound bombs. The Japanese officers overseeing the gas-for-rice exchange jumped free of their car just before the .50-caliber machine guns of the American planes chewed it to pieces. The aircraft then turned their attention to the car belonging to the local Macanese officials cutting the deal with the Japanese. Fortunately, the Macanese bailed out in time and survived the strafing of their automobile.

While the destruction of the fuel supplies could be explained from a military standpoint, a second American bombing raid later that day appeared to be more indiscriminate. Naval aircraft hit local homes, an electrical power station, a Catholic mission, and the radio station. Later raids in February and June did further damage to civilian targets, the goal apparently being to destroy anything the Japanese might find useful in a last-ditch defense of southern China.

Portuguese military forces in Macau had no anti-aircraft weapons beyond a few outdated machine guns. They quite wisely chose not to resist the American attacks, so no planes were ever hit much less shot down. Unfortunately, however, accounts suggest that at least two civilians died as a result of the raids, with many more injured.

The Portuguese government protested the American attacks, as they clearly violated Portugal's

neutrality. An American delegation eventually arrived in Macau to evaluate the damage done by the raids. In 1950 the United States paid reparations of US$20 million to the Portuguese government, though no resident of Macau ever received any direct compensation.

Like an endnote tucked away at the end of a long history book, the American raids have faded into obscurity. So too has the British occupation of Macau in 1808 during the Napoleonic Wars, when Great Britain sought to keep Macau under the control of its weak Portuguese ally rather than its formidable French enemy. Ironically, however, the Dutch invasion of 1622 remains well known even though it occurred nearly two centuries before the British occupation and some 323 years before the American bombings—probably because the Hollanders got a sound thrashing, whereas the British landed unopposed and the Americans clearly won the first and only aerial battle for Macau.

Is it Macau, Macao, or Something Else?

Very few of the world's largest cities can boast as many different names as tiny little Macau.

Macau
The original Portuguese and Macanese Patua spelling, which is also preferred by most North Americans (which is why we use it here in this book).

Macao
An alternate spelling generally used in British English and by many speakers of English outside North America.

Macau Special Administrative Region (usually shortened to Macau SAR or MSAR)
Official name for post-handover Macau.

Ou Mun
The name for Macau in Cantonese, the Chinese dialect spoken by most people in Macau. Ou Mun can be translated as "Trading Gate," or more literally, "Door of the Bay."

Aomen
The name for Macau in Mandarin, the northern or Beijing dialect of Chinese.

A Ma Gao
Cantonese for Bay of A Ma, the name local fishermen were using for Macau when the Portuguese first arrived in the sixteenth century. According to legend, the Portuguese corrupted the Cantonese A Ma Gao into Macau.

The City of the Name of God, Macau, There Is None More Loyal
Official title bestowed on Macau by the King of Portugal in 1654 in recognition of the colony's refusal to accept the 60-year Spanish occupation of Portugal.

Monte Carlo of the Orient
Clichéd title for Macau that pops up in virtually every news story and travel article ever written about the city.

Las Vegas of Asia or Vegas of the East
Up and coming cliché names for Macau.

Weed from Catholic Europe
Poet W.H. Auden's description of Macau in the 1930s

*The Macau ferry terminal combines the chaos of an invasion beachhead
with the excitement of an international airport arrivals hall.*

You are aboard the jetfoil *Sao Jorge*, which knifes through the waters of Hong Kong at high speed. Thirty minutes out from the Shun Tak Centre ferry terminal, the *Sao Jorge* passes the mountainous bulk of Lantau Island. Clouds swath the island's highest peaks, but on a lower ridgeline you spot the giant bronze Buddha of Po Lin Monastery. Freighters, ferries, fishing boats, tugs, barges, and police boats sweep past in a never-ending nautical parade down one of the world's busiest sea lanes. Overhead, sleek green-and-white helicopters race towards Macau. Soon your jetfoil slices across the invisible maritime boundary between Hong Kong and mainland China, which slowly comes into view on the horizon as a hazy, undulating line of low mountains.

Your entire body vibrates with the throb of the powerful engines as you settle into your cushioned seat, fold down your tray table, and fill out a disembarkation card with trilingual directions in Chinese, English, and a strangely out of place Portuguese. Around you pulses a microcosm of Hong Kong—middle-aged women with jade bracelets on their wrists, businessmen with briefcases and gold pens, children with Hello Kitty backpacks, and foreign tourists with sunburned expressions of befuddled wonder. Collectively they slurp tea from drink boxes, slap open pages of the *South China Morning Post*, spit energetically into motion sickness bags, and engage in mobile-phone conversations so loud it almost seems they are trying to shout across the waves separating them from their callers back in Hong Kong.

As the *Sao Jorge* heaves gently over the swells, you watch the low grey smudge of mainland China begin to take on a more distinct form. Low mountains serrate the morning sky, and you know you are seeing exactly what the first Portuguese mariners saw when they reached Macau at the dawn of the sixteenth century. A few minutes later you make out the

Lead photo description on page 191

control tower of Macau's international airport—which those pioneering Portuguese sailors most definitely did not see—and then the graceful white undulation of the Ponte de Amizade (Friendship Bridge) connecting the city center with Taipa Island. Soon the waters turn from the deep ocean blue of the shipping lanes to the olive-brown of Macau's shallow coastal waters. The white lighthouse atop Guia Hill—a famous city landmark—beckons the ferry towards the end of your 40-mile, one-hour journey.

By the time the *Sao Jorge* has slowed to coast smoothly under the Friendship Bridge, the cabin has filled with the nervous, anticipatory energy of arrival. Your fellow passengers have all grabbed their bags and started pushing for the doors. Most of them are Cantonese from Hong Kong, but some are returning Macau residents, and a few even hail from mainland China. A sprinkling of other Asian nationalities, as well as Australians, Europeans, and North Americans, further rounds out the international cast of characters. This motley invasion force comes armed with passports and identity cards, water bottles, digital cameras, mobile phones, and cash for the Hungry Tigers—as the locals call Macau's voracious casino slot machines. The HeliExpress chopper landing on the roof of the approaching ferry terminal adds to the almost martial feel of your arrival, as does the brownish haze of smog that resembles the lingering smoke of battle.

The *Sao Jorge* nudges up against the terminal pier like a man embracing an old friend. At the adjacent docks you can see a fleet of Turbojet ferries with Macanese names—*Taipa*, *Pico*, and *Penha*—and just down the coast you can see the surreal bulk of the artificial volcano that dominates Stanley Ho's new Fishermen's Wharf entertainment complex. The engine throb of your ferry fades as the crowd sways with the rock of the deck. Garbled announcements over the PA tell you something in a language that might be English or might be Cantonese—it's impossible to tell. To further the confusion, the windows of the ferry blur with water as the crew begins hosing off the salt spray. Suddenly a crewman shoves open the door and you smell a mix of diesel exhaust and salt air. With a collective cry of excitement, the crowd surges down a tubular gangway and into the terminal.

Chaos reigns inside the terminal as gamblers, businessmen, and tourists attempt to sort through the multilingual signs in Chinese, English, and Portuguese—*Bem vindo a Macau!*—while simultaneously listening to the incomprehensible announcements coming from the PA system. Skirmish lines of arriving passengers weave down the long hallways, bursting past the duty-free stores and posters advertising casinos and hotels. Lines form at passport control, where police officers in blue uniforms watch the approaching crowd with bored expressions.

You join a line beneath a sign that says "Visitors" and shuffle forward with Hong Kong Chinese toting shopping bags and answering mobile phones with a shouted *wei?* Another sign tells you that you must "Put off your cap" for a thermal temperature reading by a video camera-like device mounted over the passport control desk. If you have a fever, medical staff will pull you aside for an evaluation. After narrowly averting the SARS epidemic in 2003, Macau is taking no chances with bird flu. Your body temperature is normal, and you soon reach the head of the line. You hand over your passport, get a cursory glance from the immigration police officer, and hear his stamp whack down on your passport like a judge's gavel. You take your passport and strut into the terminal with a victor's stride.

The sunlit terminal reminds you of an international airport, with its big flashing screen listing arrival times and departure gates. You wade through the colliding currents of language— the high-decibel Cantonese, the sharp vowels of Australian

English, the old-world babble of Portuguese. The baggage claim area, currency exchange booth, tourist information office, and waiting ranks of taxis all add to the airport-like atmosphere, as does the used boarding pass stuck in your passport. You follow the flow of arriving passengers, which passes through knots of departing travelers like two colliding schools of fish. The automatic doors swish open and you step out into the hot Macau morning with a smile. You have arrived.

Ferry Facts

Ferry	Notes
Jetfoil	These single-hull vessels were built by a company that normally manufactures airliners, so it comes as no surprise that they virtually fly over the water on three waterjet-powered hydrofoil blades.

Builder	Length	Tonnage	Max Speed	Passengers
Boeing (USA)	89 feet (27 m)	267 tons (271,000 kg)	45 knots (52 mph / 84 kph)	240

Ferry	Notes
Flying Cat	These sleek, twin-hulled catamarans from a Norwegian shipyard are a common sight in the waters of Hong Kong and Macau.

Builder	Length	Tonnage	Cruise Speed	Passengers
Kvaerner / Fjellstrand (Norway)	131 feet (40 m)	479 tons (435,000 kg)	35 knots (40 mph / 64 kph)	303

Ferry	Notes
Foil Cat	One of the fastest of the ferry types, these twin-hulled catamarans rise out of the water on stubby hydrofoils mounted fore and aft on each hull.

Builder	Length	Tonnage	Cruise Speed	Passengers
Kvaerner / Fjellstrand (Norway)	115 feet (35 m)	561 tons (570,000 kg)	50 knots (58 mph / 93 kph)	399 to 419

Ferry	Notes
PS-30 Jetfoil	These Chinese-built vessels use Rolls-Royce Allison and Rockwell propulsion systems, allowing them to stand above the waves on a trio of hydrofoil blades.

Builder	Length	Tonnage	Max Speed	Passengers
Shanghai Simno Marine LTD (China)	92 feet (28 m)	303 tons (308,000 kg)	45 knots (52 mph / 84 kph)	260 to 268

Ferry	Notes
Tricat	These triple-hulled catamarans come from Britain, a country with a long maritime history in Hong Kong and Macau.

Builder	Length	Tonnage	Max Speed	Passengers
FBM Babcock Marine (United Kingdom)	154 feet (47 m)	605 tons (615,000 kg)	50 knots (58 mph / 93 kph)	303

Left: The high-speed hydrofoil Penha *speeds towards Macau.*
Right: The Penha *makes the return trip to Hong Kong.*

EXPLORING THE THREE
DISTRICTS OF MACAU ON FOOT

*Macau may well be one of the most pedestrian-friendly cities in Asia,
so be sure to bring a pair of comfortable walking shoes.*

Macau's compact nature lends itself to foot-powered exploration. Unless it is raining or unbearably hot—or both simultaneously—you can easily walk to virtually any destination. After all, if you strolled the entire length of the Macau peninsula you would only cover five miles (8.5 km).

Many of Macau's streets are geared for pedestrians rather than automobiles. The oldest streets predate the combustion engine by nearly four centuries, so they tend to be too narrow for cars. Eccentric twists and turns augmented by staircases and unexpected dead ends further bar these roads to four-wheeled traffic.

Even the newer areas of town have been designed with pedestrians in mind, however, because the locals like to walk. They walk to market and to work; they walk for exercise and for simple pleasure. Consequently many streets are pedestrian-only zones, and those that aren't usually have sidewalks. Park benches, meanwhile, are easy to find whenever you need to take a break.

Since most streets are relatively narrow, you can generally cross them without difficulty. You do not have to weave through mazes of pedestrian bridges and tunnels just to cross the street, as you often have to do in Hong Kong. You do not have to run across twelve-lane gauntlets like you do in Bangkok, either. Often you will not even have to worry about crossing the street. The old city center features many pedestrian-only thoroughfares, for example, and the traditional villages on Taipa and Coloane remain a warren of alleyways too narrow for anything larger than a motorbike.

The guaranteed presence of a street sign at every corner, no matter how small or insignificant, ensures that you are unlikely to make many wrong turns. Macau's trademark street signs consist of white porcelain tiles with blue Portuguese lettering. They would not look out of place on a Lisbon *avenida*, except that the street name is also given in Chinese characters. These

Lead photo description on page 191

beautiful blue-and-white street signs lend a touch of old-world class and charm to even the drabbest of neighborhoods and are a testament to Macau's fine aesthetic sense.

To further guide your perambulations, be sure to pick up a free map from the Macau Government Tourist Office (MGTO) in the ferry terminal when you arrive. Between the free maps and the street signs, you are unlikely to get lost in Macau. (*See pgs. 174 and 178 for more details on MGTO and the maps.*)

Even when hiking the hillside trails out on the islands of Taipa and Coloane you will run little risk of going astray. The well-maintained trails are clearly marked with directional signs, distances are short, and you can usually see a prominent landmark in the distance like the Friendship Bridge or Macau Tower to guide you along. (*See "Hiking in Macau" on pg. 136 for more about treks in the great outdoors.*)

Even if you do lose your way on the wooded slopes of Taipa or Coloane, however, you can always ask your fellow hikers and joggers for directions. Whether on the trails or the sidewalks, you will generally find that the locals are friendly and, because their city is so small, able to direct you to anyplace you want to go. Keep in mind that though many residents speak some English, most do not, so you may have to communicate by smiling, waving your arms about, and pointing at your trilingual Chinese, Portuguese, and English map from the MGTO. Knowing a word or two of Cantonese can work wonders, too. (*See "Learning the Local Lingo" on pg. 114 for more on Cantonese.*)

Macau's low crime rate also makes it a very walkable city where you will not feel the need to look over your shoulder. Bag-snatching and other street crime targeting foreign tourists remains rare; violent crime involving foreigners is even rarer, unless they are foreign gangsters. While triad gang violence associated with the casinos remains an unfortunate feature of the enclave, it occurs largely in the shadows. Basically, you can feel secure walking virtually anywhere in Macau by day. At night the streets are safe as well, though as in any city normal precautions should be taken. Walking down the proverbial dark alley at midnight is a very, very bad idea.

Traffic presents the only real danger to pedestrians in Macau, though local drivers are reasonably sane and, in any case, often reduced to second-gear speeds by narrow, twisting roads. Whether in first or fifth gear, however, local drivers always assume they have the right of way over pedestrians. The mysterious exception to this rule is the crosswalk at Senate Square, where drivers obey some unwritten point of etiquette and stop for anyone trying to cross Avenida de Almeida Ribeiro. Just about anywhere else in the city you should be cautious when crossing the street, though this advice assumes you know which way to look before stepping off the curb. Visitors from North America and continental Europe *must* remember that Macau took its automotive cue from Hong Kong rather than Portugal, which means the city drives on the British side of the road. Look right when your instincts tell you to look left.

The extreme heat and humidity of the summer months present another challenge. A one-block stroll can leave you in a sheen of sweat and desperate for a shower and change of clothes. Unlike Hong Kong—comparisons to that former British colony are inevitable when discussing Macau—where you can always find an air-conditioned public space to cool down in, Macau offers few opportunities to escape the heat. The simple truth is that in high summer, Macau is too hot to handle.

If you can, visit Macau during the cooler months from October to March. If you must visit during the summer, you can beat the heat with a few simple strategies. Wear a hat and light-colored clothing. Keep in mind that a lightweight pair of pants or long skirt is cooler in the direct sun than shorts. Do like the local women and carry an umbrella to ward off the sun—not to mention those torrential summer downpours. Drink as much water as possible, supplemented if necessary by popular sports drinks like the memorably named Pocari Sweat. Plan your day so that you walk during the cooler early morning and early evening hours, but are inside during the blistering midday hours—the air-conditioned Macau Museum is a good place to spend a summer afternoon, for example. And above all else, don't hesitate to hail a taxi or catch a bus when you feel yourself at risk of a meltdown.

Macau's taxi fleet offers a quick and hassle-free way to get around. All cabs have meters with posted rates, which are quite reasonable. Even fares out to the islands are relatively inexpensive, especially when split between several passengers. A campaign to teach drivers English has not met with great success, so be prepared to explain where you want to go by pointing at your trilingual map.

Macau's two competing bus companies also provide frequent service to most points in the city, though figuring out the routes can be quite a challenge. The buses tend to be rather small, since many city streets are too narrow to accommodate larger vehicles—and some can't accommodate vehicles of *any* size. The buses are particularly convenient for rides to/from the ferry terminal or out to the islands. (*See pg. 175 for more details on taxis and buses in Macau.*)

THE THREE DISTRICTS OF MACAU

The chapters that follow describe where to walk in each district of Macau. Essentially, each chapter provides the directions and background information necessary for self-guided walking tours (though nearly all points on these tours can be accessed by taxi or bus as well). I have designed these walking tours to take you to Macau's most well-known landmarks via some of the city's most interesting streets. In addition to the sites on the walking tour itineraries, each chapter also describes additional points of interest not on any of the walking tour routes. Armed with this information, you can devise your own route, skipping landmarks not of interest to you and adding those that are.

At some point during your trip to Macau be sure to put away your map as well as this guidebook and just let your feet go wherever they want. Macau is a great city for wandering, and you are certain to make unexpected discoveries—a backstreet temple, a secret garden, a hole-in-the-wall restaurant, a seldom-seen view of the harbor. Regardless of whether you follow the suggested routes or simply choose to wander without destination, however, be sure to walk in all three of the districts of Macau.

The Cantonese consider three to be a lucky number, so it strikes me as fortuitous indeed that Macau consists of a trio of interlinked but nonetheless distinctly separate districts. For the sake of convenience and clarity, I have opted to divide Macau into the three districts of peninsular Macau, Taipa Island, and Coloane Island. When completed, the COTAI Strip gambling district situated on reclaimed land between Coloane and Taipa will require me to divide Macau into four districts in later editions of this guidebook. At any rate, you should know that officially Macau is divided into just two districts—the peninsula and the islands— each with its own mayor. That said, Macau residents nonetheless draw distinctions between the three different parts of their city.

Macau's first district encompasses the highly urbanized Macau peninsula, which connects directly to the Chinese mainland. The second district, Taipa Island, functions as Macau's suburb; it is also the site of its international airport. Three bridges link it to the Macau peninsula. Coloane Island, which serves as Macau's countryside, makes up the third district. Reclaimed land connects it to Taipa Island. Any visit to Macau should include all three areas, starting with the history-laden Macau peninsula.

The Top Ten Things to See and Do in Macau
Here is my casino-free list of must-sees and must-dos for any first-time visitor to Macau.

1. Senate Square
Start your visit with a walk across this Portuguese-style plaza located in the heart of old Macau.

2. Ruins of St. Paul's Church
Your visit to Macau won't be complete without a pilgrimage to the city's most well-known landmark.

3. Tercena Street
You will find great browsing in the narrow lanes and alleys of this traditional neighborhood.

4. Pousada de Sao Tiago
Enjoy a carafe of *vinho verde* on the terrace of this unique hotel, which sits atop the battlements of a colonial fortress.

5. Macau Museum
If you only visit one museum in Macau, this is the one, as it offers a comprehensive overview of Macau's history and culture.

6. A-Ma Temple
Visit this temple (or any temple, for that matter) to gain a deeper understanding of Macau's complex religious history.

7. Taipa House Museum
These pastel-green villas capture the flavor of a bygone age and have become one of the city's most photographed landmarks.

8. Coloane Village
Get yourself good and lost as you wander the most traditional village in Macau, complete with tiny main square and streets too narrow for cars.

9. Macanese Cuisine
Make sure you eat a long, leisurely meal with plenty of wine at one of the city's many fine Macanese restaurants.

10. Egg Tarts
You can grab these inexpensive little delights from one of the city's many bakeries for a quick takeout snack.

One of Macau's signature tiled street signs points the way on Taipa Island.

Steps lead up the steep slopes of Taipa Grande Hill on Taipa Island.

THE MACAU PENINSULA

*The narrow streets of old Europe meet the equally narrow lanes of old China on
a three-mile-long peninsula jam-packed with nearly a half-million souls.*

Most of Macau's 465,000 residents live on the pint-sized Macau peninsula, making it one of the most densely populated areas in Asia. According to the most recently available figures from the Macau Cartography and Cadastre Bureau, the peninsula totaled just 3.4 square miles (8.8 sq. km) as of 2004. Each year land-reclamation schemes increase the peninsula's total landmass, so by the time you read this guidebook the 2004 figure will be quite outdated. The exact square mileage isn't important anyhow—all you need to know is that the peninsula is very, very small. The crowd-phobic should brace themselves, for this urban warren combines the narrow streets of old Europe with the equally narrow lanes of old China.

Despite its small size, the Macau peninsula contains the central business district, the majority of government agencies and offices, the most famous casinos, the border crossing into mainland China, and the all-important ferry terminal. It also contains most of the enclave's historic streets and buildings, including the famous and much-photographed Senate Square and iconic ruins of St. Paul's Church. The peninsula also hosts most of the museums, chief among them the Macau Museum. There is so much to see and do, in fact, that it's hard to know where to start.

The four walks described below are designed to help you with this dilemma. These walks focus on the major highlights of the peninsula that any visitor should try to see. I have organized these highlights into four separate walks—one for the middle of the peninsula, two for its southern tip, and one for the eastside NAPE on the Outer Harbor. I have also included a few additional highlights—the Macau Tower, for example—that do not readily fit into any of the four walks. If you have only a limited amount of time in Macau, I recommend the first half of the Macau Peninsula Walk from Senate Square to Camoes Garden. Combine this with the Four Largos Walk from the A-Ma Temple to Senate Square. These two relatively short walks will take in many of the city's most famous landmarks, including Senate Square, St. Paul's Church, St. Augustine's Square, and the A-Ma Temple.

When planning your exploration of the Macau peninsula, keep in mind that on Mondays and Tuesdays many museums and historic sites are closed. See below for details on opening hours.

Lead photo description on page 191

THE MACAU PENINSULA WALK

A stroll across the middle of the Macau peninsula lets you explore some of the city's most famous landmarks, including the tiled Senate Square, ruins of St. Paul's Church, and Guia Hill lighthouse.

Senate Square (Largo do Senado)

Anyone visiting Macau should start at Senate Square, which like everything else in Macau is just a short bus or taxi ride from the ferry terminal. The square opens onto Avenida de Almeida Ribeiro, a street first laid out in 1920 and by Macau standards a rather recent addition to the city. This explains why the Cantonese call the avenue San Ma Lo (New Street). This busy thoroughfare bisects the peninsula and serves as a sort of Macanese main street running through the downtown business district known as *Centro da Cidade* (the city center).

The pedestrian-only Senate Square has been lovingly restored with mosaic tiles imported from Portugal, which are arranged in wavy black-and-white swirls symbolizing the sea and Macau's maritime heritage. Arcaded colonial buildings, some dating to the 1600s, hem the square. In all of Macau, this may be the place that most completely replicates Portugal, as no matter what direction you face, you see pastel-colored colonial architecture. Of course, many of the signs are in Cantonese, and a Starbucks serves café lattes under the arcades of one venerable old building, but the overall feel still remains distinctly southern European rather than Chinese.

The white **Civic and Municipal Affairs Bureau** (circa 1784) sits at the southern end of Senate Square across the busy Avenida de Almeida Ribeiro. The building is often still referred to by its original name, Leal Senado (Loyal Senate building). This name stemmed from King Joao IV's 1654 recognition of Macau's refusal to recognize Spanish sovereignty during that country's 60-year occupation of Portugal in the seventeenth century. The original plaque bearing King Joao's proclamation of Macau's loyalty can still be seen inside the council building; however, other accounts suggest the building officially received its "Loyal" title from King John VI in 1809 as a reward for the city's victory over the much-feared Chinese pirate Kam Pau Sai. The point remains clear enough in any case—the government of colonial Macau maintained faithful

THE MACAU PENINSULA WALK

The Macau Peninsula Walk

1. Senate Square
2. Civic and Municipal Affairs Bureau
3. Holy House of Mercy
4. St. Dominic's Church & Treasure of Sacred Art Museum
5. Ruins of St. Paul's Church & Crypt and Sacred Art Museum
6. Old city walls & Na Tcha Temple
7. Monte Fort & Macau Museum
8. Luis de Camoes Garden

9. Casa Garden & Protestant Cemetery
10. Cemetery of St. Michael
11. Lou Lim Ioc Garden
12. Kun Iam Temple
13. Jardim da Montanha Russa
14. Victory Gardens
15. Dr. Sun Yat-Sen Memorial House
16. Flora Gardens & cable cars
17. Guia Hill Lighthouse

Additional Points of Interest

18. Rua da Felicidade
19. Riquexo restaurant

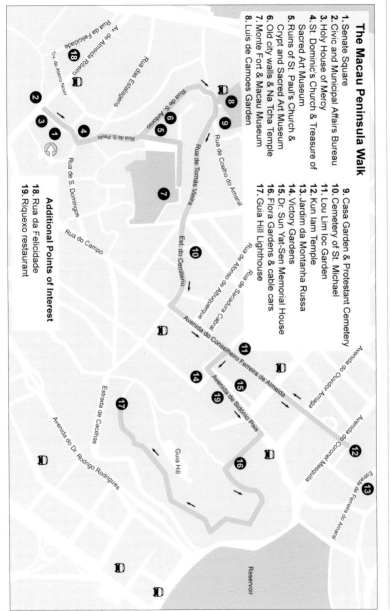

allegiance to the mother country throughout its long history. After the handover to China, however, the building lost its title and became the much plainer Civic and Municipal Affairs Bureau. Apparently Beijing did not want anyone doubting where Macau's loyalties should now rest. Be sure to duck inside the front entrance and climb the main stairs up a blue-and-white tiled passage to a charming courtyard garden. *(Open 9 a.m. to 9 p.m. Closed Mondays. Admission free.)*

The whitewashed **Holy House of Mercy** (Santa Casa da Misericordia) stands on one side of the square beside the venerable Pharmacia Popular, a vintage drugstore with an old colonial exterior and a renovated interior. The much-photographed lane between the buildings dead-ends at a bust of Bishop Carneiro, founder of the Holy House of Mercy. Established in 1569, the Holy House is the oldest Catholic charity in Macau. A museum inside the building chronicles the history of the charity, which was modeled on a similar organization in Portugal. *(Open 10 a.m. to 5:30 p.m. Closed Sundays and holidays. Admission MOP$5.)*

The far end of Senate Square blends into a smaller plaza featuring the yellow-colored **St. Dominic's Church**, which dates to the early 1600s and incorporates baroque features with local elements like

Chinese roof tiles and teak doors. The plaza itself once served as a graveyard for the earliest colonial citizens of Macau, though these days it serves more as a place for the locals to sit and gab on park benches. **The Treasure of Sacred Art Museum** chronicles the renovation of the church and contains works of religious art from various Portuguese colonies. *(Open daily 10 a.m. to 6 p.m. Admission free.)*

Standing in the square and facing St. Dominic's Church, bear right and walk a short distance to the Haagen-Dazs. Turn left on Rua da Palha, then right on the aptly named Rua de Sao Paulo. From there you can stroll up to the ruins of St. Paul's Church, Macau's most famous landmark. The narrow streets leading to St. Paul's are tiled in the same design as Senate Square, so just follow the tiles and you won't get lost. On the way to St. Paul's you will pass an assortment of colonial buildings and balconied Chinese shophouses, some of which house antique stores selling furniture from all across mainland China. You will also pass shops selling Macanese cookies and sausage. The shop staff often stand in the street offering free samples, so be sure to taste the goods.

❖   ❖   ❖

Ruins of St. Paul's Church

Given Macau's relatively blessed existence free of major calamity, I find it ironic that the enclave's most well-known building is a church gutted by fire during a typhoon. In 1835 the Jesuit-built St. Paul's Church erupted in flames, the conflagration fanned by howling storm winds. Since the Jesuits had been booted from Macau many decades before St. Paul's burned, nobody bothered to rebuild the hilltop church. Over the centuries the hollowed-out ruins became a local landmark visible from all over Macau.

Since modern buildings now shield St. Paul's from view, you are likely to first see the church when you turn a corner on pedestrian-only Rua de Sao Paulo. The elaborate façade of the church, complete with the Virgin, angels, the devil, and a Chinese dragon, waits silently at the top of a wide flight of stone steps. The effect can be somewhat eerie, for as you walk up the stairs you can see open sky through the empty door and window frames. These openings almost look like portals to heaven—an impression somewhat reduced by the pigeon-droppings smearing the heads of the saints carved into the façade.

Despite its considerable artistic merit, the Jesuits ultimately designed the façade of St. Paul's to serve a practical purpose. The carved figures and symbols on the façade collectively told a visual story of Catholicism to an illiterate Chinese audience that could not speak Portuguese or Latin. In what became known as the sermon in stone, the Jesuits preached on the steps of the church while using the imposing pictographic façade behind them to help impart the main points of Catholicism to a local audience.

The Jesuits wanted their church to be the most imposing building in Macau, and despite the disastrous fire, their wish has largely come true. After all, the ruins of St. Paul's have become Macau's most famous landmark, beating out even the neon-lit casinos. Featured in every tourist brochure and even on five and ten-pataca coins, the church serves as a symbol of the long Portuguese presence in Macau as well as the unsuccessful Jesuit attempt to Catholicize China. *(Ruins of St. Paul's open 24/7. Admission free.)*

If you want to learn more about this attempt, descend into the **Crypt and Sacred Art Museum** located behind and below the façade of St. Paul's. Inside this museum you will find a crypt containing the holy bones of martyred Vietnamese and Japanese converts to Catholicism. The crypt also contains the tomb of father Alessandro Valignano, original founder of St. Paul's and the adjoining Jesuit college. In the adjacent gallery you will find a treasure-trove of Catholic art belonging to the Macau diocese, including paintings, incense censers, chalices, icons, and crucifixes. *(Museum open daily 9 a.m. to 6 p.m. Admission free.)*

City Walls, Na Tcha Temple, and Remains of St. Paul's College

Behind and to the left of St. Paul's Church, look for a portal running through a section of the original city walls—one of only two segments remaining in Macau. Like many of Macau's earliest fortifications, this section of wall is built of *chunambo*, also known as *taipa*, a mixture of clay, straw, sand, crushed limestone, and oyster shells tightly compacted in layers between strips of wood. Although this concoction sounds flimsy, one account claims that demolishing a 460-foot (140 m) section of wall required 1,800 pounds (816 kg) of gunpowder.

Next to the city walls you will also find a small shrine dating to 1888 that honors Na Tcha, the monkey warrior of Chinese legend. No doubt the martial Na Tcha must be greatly pleased to find his temple beside the old city battlements. For visitors to Macau, however, the contrast with the nearby ruins of Catholic St. Paul's borders on the surreal. *(Open daily 8 a.m. to 5 p.m. Admission free, but donations welcome.)*

Just across the cobblestone road to the right of St. Paul's Church you can see some nondescript foundation stones unearthed in an archaeological dig. These stones mark the site of St. Paul's College, a Jesuit institution and the first Western university in Asia. In 1835 the college went up in flames along with St. Paul's Church, taking with it what may have been the most extensive Western library in Asia at that time.

Monte Fort (Fortaleza de Monte) and Macau Museum

Macau's designers and architects have a flair for putting old buildings to new uses. They do this in a way that preserves the history and architecture of the original structure, yet simultaneously allows the building to take on a new function with style and grace. Nowhere is this more apparent than in the Macau Museum, which has been built atop the battlements of the old Monte Fort directly to the right of St. Paul's Church.

If you only go to one museum in Macau, this should be the one. In a city studded with stellar museums, the Macau Museum stands out as particularly excellent. Its location inside the battlement walls gives the museum an appropriately historic feel, while the three floors of exhibits emphasize both the Chinese and the Portuguese contributions to the city's history.

Be sure to step outside the museum onto the battlements of Monte Fort for panoramic views of the city and St. Paul's Church. The fort's cannons still stand watch, though they only saw action once when the Dutch—a rival colonial power—attacked Macau in 1622. According to legend, a particularly martial Jesuit priest sent a cannonball into the Dutch powder supply, which caused an explosion sufficient to rout the invaders.

The museum's gift shop offers a good selection of books, maps, and other items related to Macau. A café by the main entrance to the museum serves drinks and snacks; however, a more atmospheric refreshment option can be found at Porta d'Armas da Fortaleza, the old gate leading into the fortress grounds. You can reach the gate by following the trail that runs around the base of the battlement walls. Pass through the gate and you will find a small, little-known café tucked away inside the ramparts. This café is a good place for a quiet cup of coffee, which you can sip while surrounded by an historic ambience of fortress walls, Portuguese fountains, and shady trees. Be sure to continue on to the upper level of the ramparts, with their cannons, casements, and commanding views of the city. In the summer, you will catch a cooling sea breeze. *(Museum open 10 a.m. to 6 p.m. Closed Mondays. Admission MOP$15. Fortress grounds open daily 7 a.m. to 7 p.m. Admission free.)*

Luis de Camoes Garden, Casa Garden, and Protestant Cemetery

From the Macau Museum, return to St. Paul's Church, head down the staircase and turn right on Rua de Santo Antonio. If you like, stop to browse in the numerous antique shops along the way. The cobblestone street eventually doglegs to the right and meets a small plaza. St. Anthony's Church stands on one side of the plaza; the Camoes Garden, Casa Garden, and a Protestant chapel and cemetery—itself a garden of sorts—front the opposite side.

Camoes Garden takes its name from a famous sixteenth-century Portuguese poet who supposedly visited the colony and penned some of his most celebrated works there. A rock grotto houses a bust of the well-traveled poet, but the park's peaceful greenery remains the real draw. The locals use the hilltop gardens for everything from gossip sessions to *tai chi* lessons, so the park offers some great people-watching opportunities. The hill's original boulders, some as large as small buildings, have been artfully integrated into the park's design. Winding paths, flower beds, groves of bamboo, and a lookout point with views across the harbor to the mainland all make a visit to the park a restful experience. *(Open daily 6 a.m. to 9:30 p.m. Admission free.)*

The Camoes Garden blends into the adjacent Casa Garden, site of a restored colonial mansion (circa 1770) that once housed the headquarters of the British East India Company, a massive international corporation specializing in illegal narcotics. This opium-dealing enterprise decamped to Hong Kong in the 1840s, and its mansion now houses art exhibitions. Stop in to see what is on display and, if you are visiting in the summer, cool down in the air conditioning. *(Open 9:30 a.m. to 6 p.m. Closed weekends and holidays. Admission free.)*

Next to the Casa Garden stands a small Protestant chapel and cemetery, which contains the remains of British, Dutch, and American sailors, merchants, and missionaries who perished in or near Macau in the eighteenth and nineteenth centuries. Their timeworn gravestones chronicle an array of fatal dangers ranging from fever to foundering ships. Some 150 Westerners lie here, including Lord H. J. Spencer Churchill, the great-grand-uncle of Winston Churchill, and George Chinnery, the famed British painter who chronicled nineteenth-century Macau. Robert Morrison, the first Protestant missionary to China who translated the New Testament into Chinese, also lies buried here with his wife and son. With its grass lawn shaded by frangipani and bauhinia trees, the cemetery has an appropriately peaceful atmosphere. *(Open daily 9:00 a.m. to 5:30 p.m.)*

Lou Lim Ioc Garden

To reach Lou Lim Ioc Garden from Camoes Garden and the Protestant cemetery, walk down Rua de Tomas Vieira and through a traffic roundabout to Estrada do Cemiterio. Here you will pass by the **Cemetery of St. Michael the Archangel**, a graveyard fantasyland packed with Virgin Mary icons, harp-strumming angels, and assorted saints. *(Open daily 10 a.m. to 6 p.m.)* Turn left on Avenida do Conselheiro Ferreira de Almeida and walk past a series of beautifully restored colonial buildings still in use as government offices, until you reach the Lou Lim Ioc Garden on the left-hand side of the street.

To a Western visitor, the walled Lou Lim Ioc Garden might best be described as an overgrown maze with an over the top Chinese theme. The walled grounds turn the park into a secret garden with an intimate feel; the clever layout and lush greenery obscure its compact size. Built by the father of wealthy Chinese merchant Lou Lim Ioc in the late 1800s and modeled on the famous gardens of Suzhou, the grounds feature winding paths and zigzagging bridges—to confuse evil spirits, who move in straight lines—as well as bamboo groves, lotus ponds, ornate pavilions, and moon gates. Here you will have the chance to view traditional Chinese landscape design, which presents an idealized view of nature in miniature form. The park attracts practitioners of traditional Chinese arts, so expect to encounter locals playing the stringed *erhu*, waving *tai chi* swords, or dancing with crescent-shaped red fans. *(Open daily 6 a.m. to 9 p.m. Admission is a very affordable MOP$1.)*

Kun Iam Temple

When you leave the Lou Lim Ioc Garden, continue north on Avenida do Conselheiro Ferreira de Almeida for several blocks until the avenue ends at Avenida do Coronel Mesquita. Turn left on Mesquita and you will see the grounds of Macau's oldest place of worship, a temple devoted to Kun Iam, goddess of mercy. Though not as famous as the A-Ma Temple, the Kun Iam Temple nonetheless remains one of the city's most popular and prosperous places of worship. Though established in the 1400s—a century before the Catholic Portuguese arrived—the temple's oldest buildings only date back to 1627. In the main hall, an image of Kun Iam stands in elaborate embroidered silk, her head adorned with a crown changed every year by her devoted worshippers. Eighteen Chinese sages flank Kun Iam on each side; look closely and you will spot the renowned Italian adventurer Marco Polo among them.

The temple grounds feature terraced gardens complete with

shrines, fountains, and the site of the first Sino-American trade treaty. Viceroy of Canton Ki Ying and American minister Caleb Cushing— who went on to become U.S. attorney general under President Franklin Pierce—signed the treaty on a stone table on this very spot in 1844. The event hardly remains cause for celebration, however, as the prostrate Chinese imperial government had just been defeated by the British and signed the American treaty against its will. On a different note, you can pray for marital fidelity at the garden's cluster of four banyans, which are collectively known as the Lovers Tree on account of their intertwined branches.

As in all places of worship in Macau, visitors are welcome. However, guests should dress appropriately and behave respectfully. Unless a sign forbids it, taking pictures is usually permitted. Always ask, however, before taking photos of someone. *(Open daily from dusk to dawn. Admission free, but donations welcome.)*

Jardim da Montanha Russa
(Snail Hill Garden)

Behind the Kun Iam Temple on Estrada de Ferreira do Amaral you can find the Jardim da Montanha Russa, a quiet retreat from the noisy streets that is known only to the locals. This little green gem occupies a wooded hill that attracts amorous young couples who clearly hope they will someday pray beneath the Lovers Tree in the nearby Kun Iam Temple. The park's name derives from the Chinese word for snail, which evokes the way the main path spirals up the hill to a platform offering views of the surrounding city. A small café serves up various snacks and caffeinated beverages, so if you want to take a break in an authentic neighborhood park that seldom sees foreign tourists, then the Jardim da Montanha Russa is the green space for you. *(Open daily 6 a.m. to 10 p.m. Admission free.)*

Dr. Sun Yat-Sen Memorial House

Retrace your route back to the Lou Lim Ioc Garden and turn left on Estrada de Adolfo Loureiro. Walk one block to where the street ends at history-packed Avenida de Sidonio Pais. Directly across the road you will see the **Jardim da Vitoria—Victory Gardens**—which commemorates the Portuguese victory over a Dutch invasion force in 1622.

Turn left on Avenida de Sidonio Pais and, if you wish, stop in at the Dr. Sun Yat-Sen Memorial House. Sun Yat-Sen led a nationalist revolution that overthrew the last Chinese dynasty in 1911, and is considered a father of the nation. He resided in Macau for two years, worked as a doctor, and befriended the classical garden-enthusiast Lou Lim Ioc as well as the famous writer Zheng Guangying, whose home will soon become the Mandarin's House Museum. *(See pg. 69.)* Ironically, however, Sun Yat-Sen never lived in the memorial home that bears his name. An explosion blamed on poorly stored explosives leveled the original house on this site—a fate shared by a surprising number of buildings in Macau. In the 1930s, Sun Yat-Sen's wife and two children built the memorial house, with its blend of Moorish and Chinese architecture, to honor their husband and father. Madame Sun Yat-Sen is buried in the United Chinese Cemetery on Taipa Island. *(Open 10 a.m. to 5 p.m. Closed Tuesdays. Admission free.)*

Guia Hill Lighthouse

While not quite as famous as St. Paul's Church, the Guia Hill lighthouse remains far more visible. Standing atop the highest point on the peninsula, the white lighthouse can be seen from many points along the eastern side of the city as well as from the harbor and out to sea—not to mention the flipside of one-pataca coins.

The lighthouse has become one of Macau's most beloved landmarks and a symbol of its maritime heritage. It has been in service since 1865, though a typhoon put it out of action for a period in the late 1800s. Today the white tower's beacon continues to guide fishermen and ferry captains, who on clear days can see its familiar flash from up to 20 miles (32 km) out to sea. The flag pole beside the lighthouse still hoists storm-warning flags whenever a typhoon approaches Macau.

To reach the lighthouse, continue down Avenida de Sidonio Pais past the Sun Yat-Sen Memorial House until you see the **cable cars** that run to the top of Guia Hill. For a speedy ascent, you can ride the cable cars to the top in about 80 seconds. Alternatively, you can hike the trails that wind up the hill to the summit. On the way you will pass the **Flora Gardens**, with its small and somewhat neglected zoo. The gardens stand on the site of a mansion burned to the ground in the 1920s after a nearby fireworks factory

blew itself to bits—a not uncommon event in Macau's history. *(Flora Gardens open daily 7 a.m. to 7 p.m. Admission free. Cable cars run from 7 a.m. to 6 p.m. Tickets cost MOP$3 one-way or 5 roundtrip.)*

When you reach the top, head south along the exercise trail towards the lighthouse. Look carefully while walking the ridge-top trail and you will see old Portuguese gun emplacements hidden in the undergrowth. Eventually the city hopes to renovate these emplacements as well as the maze of military tunnels running beneath Guia Hill, which would create what might well be Macau's most unusual museum.

You will soon reach the lighthouse and its attached chapel, both of which stand atop the whitewashed battlements of the seventeenth-century Guia Fort. With its fine views and location in the largest park on the peninsula, Guia Hill lighthouse offers a pleasant respite from the clamorous city streets below—particularly in the summer, when a brisk sea breeze often blows across the hill. When you feel that cool wind on a sweltering midsummer day, you will truly wonder why the Guia Hill lighthouse only rated a place on the lowly one-pataca coin. *(Park grounds open 24/7. Chapel and fortress open 9 a.m. to 5:30 p.m. Closed Mondays. Admission free.)*

THE MACAU PENINSULA WALK

THE PRAIA GRANDE WALK

This pleasant, tree-shaded stroll takes you down one of Asia's most famous coastal promenades, complete with cannons, cathedrals, and chilled white wine.

After exploring the middle of the busy Macau peninsula, you might be ready for a more tranquil stroll down and around its southern tip. Though not as quiet as it used to be, the southern end still has a more peaceful feel to it than the more northerly points on the peninsula. This largely residential area has its share of historic sites, however, as well as a few additional surprises of the sort only Macau can dish up.

The Praia Grande

Start your walk on Senate Square and head south on Avenida de Almeida Ribeiro until you hit Avenida da Praia Grande. Turn right for a leisurely stroll along what used to be the most famous coastal promenade in Asia. The northern portion of the Praia Grande has now been swallowed by land-reclamation projects, while the southern half of the former seaside avenue fronts an artificial lake complete with giant **cybernetic fountain**. *(For more on the fountain, see the Weekend Art Fair on pg. 163.)* On the opposite side of this lake you will be able to see a triangle of reclaimed land featuring various government buildings, the convention center, and the 1,110-foot tall (338 m) Macau Tower—a modern colossus of reinforced concrete that would not look out of place in Communist-era East Berlin. Your stroll along the Praia Grande will also take you past a **monument to Jorge Alvares**, captain of the first Portuguese galleon to reach the Pearl River Delta in 1513, as well as the pastel-pink **Headquarters of the Macau SAR**, originally constructed in the 1840s for a wealthy Macanese family and later purchased by the government. If you need refreshment along the way, a very European-looking kiosk serves drinks in a triangular plaza outside the Praia Grande Restaurant.

Penha Hill

Fortresses still command all the best hilltop locations on the Macau peninsula, and even the one exception—the Chapel of our Lady of Penha atop Penha Hill—sits on the site of a former fortification. While not the most architecturally or historically interesting Catholic place of worship in Macau, you can't beat the view from the chapel's courtyard. The view, in fact, explains why a

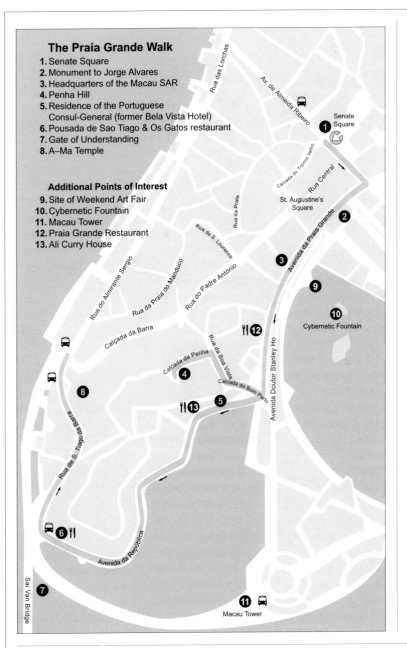

The Praia Grande Walk
1. Senate Square
2. Monument to Jorge Alvares
3. Headquarters of the Macau SAR
4. Penha Hill
5. Residence of the Portuguese
   Consul-General (former Bela Vista Hotel)
6. Pousada de Sao Tiago & Os Gatos restaurant
7. Gate of Understanding
8. A–Ma Temple

Additional Points of Interest
9. Site of Weekend Art Fair
10. Cybernetic Fountain
11. Macau Tower
12. Praia Grande Restaurant
13. Ali Curry House

fortress once crowned the 207-foot (63 m) hill. From Penha Hill you can see the Macau Tower, all three of Macau's bridges, Taipa Island, and the ferry-streaked waters of the Pearl River Delta. In turn, the chapel can be seen from all of these points and has become another well-known Macau landmark as a result. *(Chapel open daily 9 a.m. to 5:30 p.m. Admission free.)*

To reach Penha Hill from the Praia Grande, turn right on Calcada do Bom Parto just after the Municipal Children's Garden (Parque Infantil do Chunambeiro). Walk a short distance uphill and then go right on Rua da Boa Vista and left on Calcada da Penha to Penha Hill. This is a steep but pleasant walk in the winter; in the summer, you might consider cheating a bit and flagging a taxi for this part of your stroll. After taking in the view from Penha Hill, retrace your route downhill towards the Praia Grande.

Residence of the Portuguese Consul-General (former Bela Vista Hotel)

As you walk down from Penha Hill you will pass the home of the Portuguese Consul-General, where the flag of Portugal proudly ripples in the breeze blowing in from the South China Sea. The consul lives in the former Bela Vista Hotel. As its name suggests, the hotel's location gave it a sweeping view of the Pearl River Delta—a view now bisected by the omnipresent Macau Tower. Constructed atop the ramparts of the old Bom Parto fort, the opulent Bela Vista shared an elite status with a handful of old colonial hotels that included the Peninsula in Hong Kong, the Metropole in Hanoi, the Raffles in Singapore, and the Oriental in Bangkok. Sadly, only the Bela Vista has closed its doors to guests.

Pousada de Sao Tiago

Continue down from Penha Hill to the Praia Grande and turn right. Here the Praia Grande curves sharply and morphs into Avenida da Republica, where the promenade's original stone seawall still remains—though it now fronts yet another man-made lake rather than the open waters of the Pearl River Delta. Continue your stroll, passing balconied homes reminiscent of the Mediterranean, until you reach the Pousada de Sao Tiago. The pousada has always been one of my favorite hotels in Macau, both because it has been so tastefully and cleverly slotted into the ramparts of a seventeenth-century fortress and because it offers the best front door of any hotel in the world.

When the pousada's door swings open, you won't find a conventional hotel lobby. Instead you will find a stone staircase that tunnels up through the old battlements. A fountain at the top of the stairs sends water flowing down a tiled runnel alongside the steps. Entering the pousada feels like walking under a waterfall without actually getting wet, and this natural air conditioning always offers a welcome relief from the humid estuary heat.

Take a seat on the terrace of the pousada's gourmet restaurant, an alfresco affair that stands atop the time-streaked fortress walls. You will be fanned by a pleasant breeze blowing off the water and shaded by banyan trees so old they have sprouted out of the very ramparts. Do like the locals and order a carafe of *vinho verde* white wine (MOP$70) and, if hungry, some classic Macanese fare like *pasteis de bacalhau* (codfish rolls) or *galinha a Macau* (Macau chicken). Be sure to check out the pousada's little whitewashed chapel dedicated to Sao Tiago (St. James), patron saint of Portuguese soldiers.

When I first enjoyed the pousada's hospitality back in the final years of Portuguese rule, the hotel fronted on the water and offered an unobstructed view of the sleepy Inner Harbor. From the terrace of the pousada, Macau really did feel like a colonial backwater snared in some kind of Euro-Asian time warp. These days, however, time has picked up the pace, hurling both the pousada and Macau into the future with disorienting speed. The pousada's view now includes the newly constructed double-deck

bridge to Taipa Island and a highway bypass to the Macau Tower. You can also see a black monolith called the **Gate of Understanding**, a memorial dedicated somewhat wishfully to centuries of Sino-Portuguese goodwill and cooperation. You could argue all this has spoiled a once scenic view, but after a glass or two of white wine you will still find yourself slipping pleasantly into the pousada's time-warpy charm.

If you wish to continue your stroll, walk from the pousada around the tip of the peninsula along Rua de Sao Tiago da Barra, said to be the oldest street in Macau. You will soon come to the tiled A-Ma Square, starting point of the Four Largos Walk.

THE FOUR LARGOS WALK

This walk winds through a series of tiled squares that showcase the blending of Eastern and Western influences in Macau.

I highly recommend this walk, which ranks as one of my favorite strolls in Macau—or anywhere else in Asia, for that matter. I have designed this walk to be an extension of the Praia Grande Walk, which is why it begins at the A-Ma Temple. However, you could also start the Four Largos Walk at Senate Square—the first of the four *largos*—and simply walk the route backwards through St. Augustine's Square and on past Lilau Square to the plaza outside the A-Ma Temple. This might be your best option if you are not intending to walk the Praia Grande.

A-Ma Temple

In a somewhat roundabout fashion, the venerable A-Ma Temple gave Macau its name. The Chinese fishermen living in the area some 500 years ago called their home A-Ma Gao (Bay of A-Ma)—a name that the Portuguese corrupted into "Macau" when they supposedly made their first landing at this very spot. A

variant of this story holds that the Portuguese came up with the word "Macau" when they heard the local name for the temple: Ma Kok. Nobody really knows which story to believe, though I'm guessing both have some truth to them.

The red A-Ma Temple actually houses three separate temples devoted to the patron deity of seafarers, A-Ma—also known, especially in Hong Kong, as Tin Hau. A fourth temple is dedicated to the goddess of mercy Kun Iam, another protector of Macau. Both deities are worshipped by Buddhists and Taoists alike, not to mention some local Catholics.

The A-Ma Temple has been protecting Macau for at least five centuries and predates the enclave's Catholic churches. Some locals like to say that Macau's relatively blessed existence free of warfare, natural disasters, and plagues like the recent SARS epidemic, stems from the protection of three divine ladies—the Taoist A-Ma, Buddhist Kun Iam, and Catholic Lady of Fatima.

The fragrant smell of burning joss pervades the temple in a fog of grey smoke. Smoldering joss—a Cantonese word derived from *deus*, the Portuguese word for God—hangs from the temple ceilings in giant coils that do a circular slow burn. Still more joss sticks, some nearly as thick as baseball bats, stand in lucky clusters

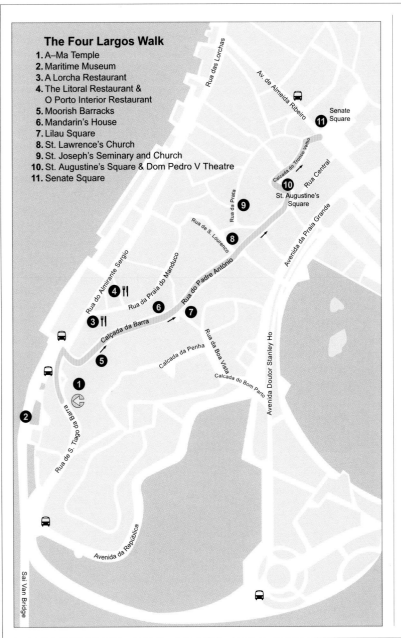

The Four Largos Walk
1. A–Ma Temple
2. Maritime Museum
3. A Lorcha Restaurant
4. The Litoral Restaurant &
   O Porto Interior Restaurant
5. Moorish Barracks
6. Mandarin's House
7. Lilau Square
8. St. Lawrence's Church
9. St. Joseph's Seminary and Church
10. St. Augustine's Square & Dom Pedro V Theatre
11. Senate Square

of three before various altars to A-Ma and other deities. Thickets of little joss sticks the size of bottle rockets supplement the larger sticks. The joss never stops burning, as worship follows no set schedule and a continual parade of locals passes through the temple gates throughout the day. They plant their joss sticks in ceremonial altar bowls while praying for good fortune, giving thanks for success, and making offerings on behalf of departed ancestors. *(Open daily from 7 a.m. to 6 p.m.)*

Maritime Museum

Cross the square outside the A-Ma Temple to the Maritime Museum, which is devoted to Macau's long heritage as an international port city. The museum houses displays devoted to South China Sea fishermen, Portuguese and Chinese voyages of discovery, maritime technology and trade, and regional marine life. Appropriately, the museum was built on the shores of the Inner Harbor more or less where the first Portuguese landed in the early 1500s. Just as appropriately, the building was designed to resemble the stylized shape of a sailing vessel. These days the museum still looks like a ship under sail, but the approach road to the new Sai Van Bridge has left the building completely landlocked. *(Open 10 a.m. to 5:30 p.m. Closed Tuesdays. Admission MOP$10.)*

As far as I can ascertain, the newly landlocked museum no longer offers cruises aboard the *A-Ma*, its vintage Chinese junk. However, inquire inside the museum in case the cruises have resumed, in which case for just ten patacas you can sail on a 30-minute junket aboard an ocean-going museum display, crewed by the husband and wife team who once lived aboard the *A-Ma* before donating it to the museum. Your cruise around the harbor will take you past fishing boats, small freighters, tugs, and barges; it will also offer views of mainland China, the new Sai Van Bridge and, inevitably, the Macau Tower.

If the Maritime Museum and the possibility of a cruise aboard the *A-Ma* pique your interest in the now-rare Chinese junks of Macau, you might consider visiting the enclave's last junk-building yard on Coloane Island. *(See pg. 125 for more details.)*

Macanese Restaurants

You might work up an appetite while sailing aboard the *A-Ma*, but it won't be for junk food. Instead you will want Macau's famous Macanese and Portuguese cuisine, which you can easily find by walking a short distance down Rua do Almirante Sergio. Here you will find a trio of three well-established restaurants—the Litoral, A Lorcha, and O Porto

Interior—clustered together on this busy street just past the A-Ma Temple. *(For more details on these restaurants, see pg. 146.)*

Moorish Barracks

Follow Calcada da Barra, a narrow street leading off from the corner of the square outside the A-Ma Temple. This street will curve to the right, bringing you to the distinctive yellow-painted Moorish Barracks (circa 1871–74). Despite the name, the barracks once housed a colonial Indian regiment from Goa. Today the building houses the Macau Maritime Administration. You are free to wander down the building's airy verandah, though only those on official business are allowed access inside the barracks itself. *(Veranda open to public 9 a.m. to 6 p.m.)*

Mandarin's House

At the point where Rua da Barra narrows to a width barely wide enough for a car, you will see the distinctive architecture of a traditional Chinese residential compound on your left. This is the former home of Zheng Guangying, a famous writer, philosopher, and businessman who befriended Dr. Sun Yat-Sen. Like Sun Yat-Sen, Zheng Guangying stands out as one of Macau's most revered Chinese historical figures, and not surprisingly, both men have avenues named after them in the NAPE district. Built in

1881, Zheng Guangying's compound blends Eastern and Western elements in a graceful fusion of the sort only Macau could come up with. At heart this is a traditional Chinese residence, however, complete with gardens and courtyards. Over the years the courtyards and interconnected houses fell into a state of disrepair, but the government of Macau has now begun restoration work. Given Macau's exceptional talent for restoring historical buildings, I have no doubts that the compound will be fully returned to its former glory. Eventually the buildings and courtyards will be opened to the public as the Mandarin's House Museum, but for the time being you can only peer over the compound's time-stained walls to get a glimpse of this marvelous old home.

Lilau Square (Largo do Lilau)

Walk a very short distance up the road until you reach Largo do Lilau. Locals know this small plaza for its natural spring, which continues to gush the same steady stream of water it did when the first Portuguese arrived in Macau. A Macanese folk saying says of the Lilau fountain:

Who drinks from the waters of Lilau can never leave Macau.
Their home is in Macau, and they will always return to Macau.

These days a sign warns that the water is not safe to drink, but hopefully you will return to Macau even without sampling the waters of Lilau.

St. Lawrence's Church

Follow the main road—which rapidly changes names several times—past Largo do Lilau. After a short distance you will reach St. Lawrence's Church with its twin steeples and forecourt of palm trees. Though the church could use an exterior paint job, and the clock on the left steeple no longer keeps time, the inside of the church is still quite impressive. If you have not already reached your quota of churches—which is rather easy to do in Macau—then stop in for a look at St. Lawrence's ornate interior. The church itself only dates to the early 1800s, but the first Catholic services took place here in the 1560s in a wooden chapel. Though modern buildings now obscure the view, the church once overlooked government house—the ornate rose-colored building that now serves as the Headquarters of the Macau SAR. Buildings and residences belonging to the opium-dealing British East India Company once neighbored the church as well. If the front gates are closed during the day, try the side gate on Rua da Imprensa Nacional. *(Open 10 a.m. to 4 p.m. Closed Mondays. Admission free, but donations welcome.)*

St. Joseph's Seminary and Church

Take Rua de Sao Lourenco on the left side of St. Lawrence's Church. Follow this road as it bends to the right behind the church and continue walking down Rua da Prata to St. Joseph's Seminary and Church. Founded by the Jesuits in 1728, the seminary played a key role in missionary activities in China. Today the seminary houses what may be Macau's most famous holy relic—a bone fragment from St. Francis Xavier's elbow. If you go inside the church, be sure to see the little walled courtyard reached by a corridor near the altar. This charming secret garden features an old well, trees, and flowering hibiscus. *(Church open 10 a.m. to 5 p.m. Admission free, but donations welcome. Seminary closed to public.)*

St. Augustine's Square (Largo de Santo Agostinho)

Return to St. Lawrence's Church and continue your walk until you reach Calcada do Teatro, which will take you up into the pleasant Largo de Santo Agostinho. Colonial buildings line this plaza on all sides, which makes the tiled square feel like a living history museum. Here you will find the back gates to St. Joseph's Seminary as well as the Sir Robert Ho Tung Public Library (circa 1894). *(Open 1 p.m. to 7 p.m. Closed Sundays.)* You will also find St. Augustine's Church, founded in 1586, though the present building dates to 1814. *(Church closed to public.)* Opposite the church stands the restored **Dom Pedro V Theatre**—a pastel-green neoclassical delight built in 1860, which makes it the oldest European theatre in China. Surprisingly, the theatre hosted the famous Crazy Paris striptease show from 1978 to 1986—an episode that seems rather beneath the dignity of such an elegant old building. These days the girls of the Crazy Paris show continue to reveal all at the appropriately gaudy Lisboa Hotel. *(Theatre and its roof garden open 10 a.m. to 11 p.m. Admission free.)* Should you need to take a break, the square features a European-style kiosk that sells drinks and snacks.

To return to Senate Square, cross St. Augustine's Square and walk down Calcada do Tronco Velho.

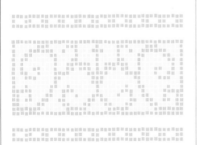

THE NAPE AND OUTER HARBOR WALK

A walk through the seaside NAPE may lack the old-world charm of downtown Macau, but it will show you the city's modern face.

Much of Macau sits on land reclaimed from the shallow Pearl River Delta. According to the Macau Cartography and Cadastre Bureau, the territory totaled just 4.5 square miles (11.6 sq. km) in 1912, but had more than doubled to 11 square miles (27.5 sq. km) by 2004. In the older sections of the city you generally can't tell when you are walking over this reclaimed land. In newer sections of the city like the NAPE, however, you will have no trouble spotting the reclaimed land for the simple reason that *all* of this district used to be open water.

The NAPE—*Novos Aterros do Porto Exterior*, or New Reclaimed Land of the Outer Harbor—is a completely artificial neighborhood where everything was carefully planned in advance and everything is new. The NAPE might lack the vitality and charm of Macau's older neighborhoods, but it is still worth a visit because it can reveal so much about what Macau

The Nape and Outer Harbor Walk

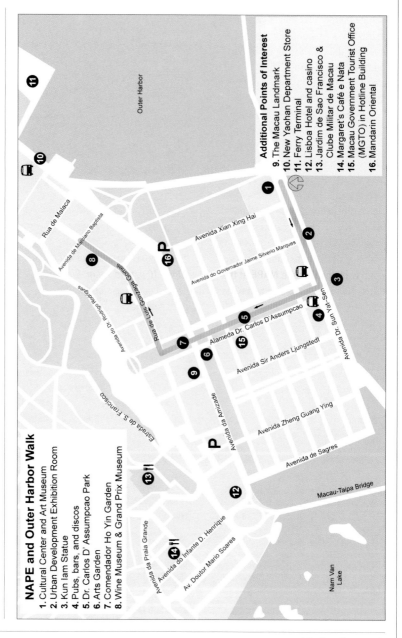

Outer Harbor

Rua de Malaca

Avenida de Marciano Baptista

Avenida de Jr. Rodrigo Rodrigues

Rua de Luis Gonzaga Gomes

Avenida Xian Xing Hai

Avenida do Governador Jaime Silverio Marques

Alameda Dr. Carlos D'Assumpcao

Avenida Sir Anders Ljungstedt

Avenida Dr. Sun Yat-Sen

Estrada de S. Francisco

Avenida da Amizade

Avenida Zheng Guang Ying

Avenida de Sagres

Macau-Taipa Bridge

Nam Van Lake

Avenida da Praia Grande

Avenida do Infante D. Henrique

Av. Doutor Mario Soares

NAPE and Outer Harbor Walk

1. Cultural Center and Art Museum
2. Urban Development Exhibition Room
3. Kun Iam Statue
4. Pubs, bars, and discos
5. Dr. Carlos D' Assumpcao Park
6. Arts Garden
7. Comendador Ho Yin Garden
8. Wine Museum & Grand Prix Museum

Additional Points of Interest

9. The Macau Landmark
10. New Yaohan Department Store
11. Ferry Terminal
12. Lisboa Hotel and casino
13. Jardim de Sao Francisco & Clube Militar de Macau
14. Margaret's Café e Nata
15. Macau Government Tourist Office (MGTO) in Hotline Building
16. Mandarin Oriental

Map Legend on page 191

values—after all, nothing wound up in the NAPE by accident. If you find something in the NAPE, you have found it because city planners put it there, from parks to pubs to porcelain street signs.

A visit to the NAPE—pronounced "NA-pay"—will also allow you to get a more well-rounded sense of the city, since not everyone lives in an old colonial home on a cobblestone street in the old quarter. Most residents, in fact, live in apartment blocks and work in modern buildings of the sort found throughout the NAPE. So while I wouldn't suggest that you put a walk through the NAPE at the top of your list, I would recommend it if you have time. After all, the NAPE is the real Macau, too.

Cultural Center and Art Museum

Start this walk at the Cultural Center, arriving by taxi to save time and energy. The Cultural Center, with its distinctive roof shaped like a ski jump, is open to the public and often hosts interesting temporary displays as well as the cream of the city's music, drama, and opera performances.

A covered walkway connects to the adjacent Art Museum, which like its sister Cultural Center, can thank its existence to all those gambling-generated tax revenues. With a 3,000-piece collection, the five-story museum has world-class ambitions. Its galleries contain permanent exhibitions of Chinese calligraphy, porcelain, bronze work, painting, and other artwork.

The Gallery of Historical Paintings contains a large number of artworks depicting life in Macau before the advent of photography. These paintings include works by George Chinnery (1774–1852), Macau's most celebrated Western painter who now lies buried in the city's old Protestant cemetery. Even if you have a limited tolerance for art museums, the displays are still worth a browse, especially on a hot day when you will love the air conditioning. *(Open 10 a.m. to 7 p.m. Closed Mondays. Admission MOP$5.)*

Kun Iam Statue

Take the pedestrian overpass that crosses Avenida Dr. Sun Yat-Sen from the Art Museum. Stop at the viewing platform on the opposite side, which offers expansive views of the Outer Harbor, then return to street level and head west along the waterfront.

On your way down Avenida Dr. Sun Yat-Sen you will pass the Macau **Urban Development Exhibition Room** with its distinctive pill-capsule shape. Built by the Land, Public Works, and Transport Bureau, this building showcases Macau's penchant for massive construction projects. If this piques your curiosity, stop in to view the scale models and other displays related to the construction of the Sai Van Bridge, the East Asian Games stadium, and other large-scale projects. *(Open Tuesday to Friday 10 a.m. to 1 p.m. and 2:30 p.m. to 6:00 p.m. Saturday and Sunday open 2 p.m. to 6 p.m. Closed Mondays. Admission free.)*

Continue down Avenida Dr. Sun Yat-Sen. This coastal boulevard on the southern edge of the NAPE serves as a modern-day Praia Grande and is dominated by a statue of Kun Iam, the goddess of mercy. This 65-foot tall (20 m) gold-colored likeness of the city's patron deity might seem a bit kitsch on first glance, but a second look reveals a graceful sculpture that stands out from the surrounding area and will no doubt eventually evolve into a city landmark as famous as the ruins of St. Paul's. That the city allowed the statue to be placed in such a prominent and high-value location says a lot about the standing of Kun Iam in Macau. *(Information hall and shop open 10 a.m. to 6 p.m. Closed Fridays. Admission free.)*

On the other hand, the restaurants, discos, cafés, and pubs found just across the street from the statue reveal the importance Macau residents place on a good night out. This purpose-built entertainment area inevitably gets compared to Hong Kong's legendarily raucous Lan Kwai Fong district and invariably comes off a poor second—but then what place

wouldn't? A fairer comparison might be to the restaurants struggling to make it on the Sanlitun terrace of Causeway Centre near Hong Kong's Wan Chai Star Ferry terminal.

All those nightspots suggest you might want to return to this area in the evening, when the floodlit Kun Iam Statue is particularly striking and the watering holes begin to fill with locals out on the town. The nearby parks, with their softer lighting, can also take on a particularly enchanting atmosphere.

Dr. Carlos D'Assumpcao Park
Walk inland from the Kun Iam statue into Dr. Carlos D'Assumpcao Park, a pleasant green space that bisects the NAPE. This park offers plenty of shaded park benches and play space for children. The value that Macau places on parks and greenery remains obvious here, given that this land could have easily been used for office towers instead.

Stroll the length of the park until you cross a main road and enter the Jardim das Artes (**the Arts Garden**). If you haven't had your fill of parks and/or you particularly enjoy brightly colored outdoor sculpture art, you can make a quick detour into the Jardim das Artes before crossing Avenida da Amizade to yet another park—**Comendador Ho Yin Garden**. (All three parks open daily 6 a.m. to 11 p.m. Admission free.)

Walk halfway up Comendador Ho Yin Garden, then turn right and go out the gate opposite Rua de Luis Gonzaga Gomes. Follow Gonzaga Gomes, walking past a parking lot full of PLA military vehicles with spit-and-polish sentries who do not welcome picture-takers. After foregoing this martial photo op, you will soon reach the rather unimaginatively named Tourism Activities Center at 60 Rua de Luis Gonzaga Gomes.

Wine Museum and Grand Prix Museum

Located inside the Tourism Activities Center (or CAT, after its Portuguese acronym), these two small museums appeal to specialized interests. Aficionados of Portuguese wine and port may find the wine museum interesting; those with a passion for motor racing specifically and cars in general may find the Grand Prix Museum interesting as well.

The wine museum is often described as the only museum in the world devoted to the history of wine-making in Portugal, though this claim is unsubstantiated. However, it is likely the only such museum in Asia. Each of the many wine-growing regions of Portugal has its own display, complete with mannequins in ethnic dress. These pale and motionless figures give the museum an atmosphere somewhere between a department store clothing section

and a haunted wax museum. Along with the mannequins, the displays feature vintage bottles of wine, antique wine-making equipment, and various gear associated with producing *vinho verde* and other types of Portuguese wine. Don't go to the museum just for the much-touted wine tasting offered with each admission ticket, however, as you will be disappointed with just one tiny thimbleful of wine and not a drop more. *(Open 10 a.m. to 6 p.m. Closed Tuesdays. Admission MOP$15.)*

Every November since 1954 the city has hosted the famous Macau Grand Prix, which actually consists of different races for Formula 3 racing cars, touring cars (known as stock cars in the USA), motorcycles, and motorbikes—this last category a homegrown sport based on local residents' love for their Honda Dreams and other motor-scooters. As in Monaco, another microstate with a Grand Prix, the race runs on a circuit pieced together from the city streets. The 3.8-mile circuit (6 km) includes the winding roads of Guia Hill, the sharp corners and hairpin turns around the reservoir, and the straightaway past the ferry terminal—a loop champion drivers can do in not much more than two minutes. The museum recounts the history of the Grand Prix and features the Triumph TR2 that won the inaugural race as well as some winning motorcycles. Interactive exhibits like race-driving simulators give you a chance to try your luck behind the wheel. Hardcore race fans might consider taking a short taxi ride over to the Grand Prix control tower near the ferry terminal, though access to the building itself is restricted. *(Open 10 a.m. to 6 p.m. Closed Tuesdays. Admission MOP$10.)*

RUA DA FELICIDADE

Take a jaunt down Happiness Street in the early evening, when Macau is at its best.

I've always felt that Macau is at its best in the early morning and early evening hours. If you are only in Macau for the day, then you won't be making any early morning strolls; however, you will have time for a nighttime walk through the backstreets of old Macau. While you could stroll from Senate Square in any direction and find a never-ending maze of enchanting backstreets, I recommend heading for the former red-light district centered around the somewhat euphemistically named Rua da Felicidade (Happiness Street).

To get to Rua da Felicidade, walk west up Avenida de Almeida Ribeiro for a short distance, then cross the street and head up the narrow Travessa do Aterro Novo. *(See map on pg. 53.)* You will quickly reach Happiness Street, so named for the houses of ill repute that once lined this narrow back lane. This was the place for those seeking opium dens—legal until 1947—and bordellos, which are still legal though no longer in action on Rua da Felicidade. Today the former bordellos have been restored to their original red-painted luster, but now host restaurants, bars, and shops instead of more shady establishments.

At night Rua da Felicidade and the adjoining streets come alive, filled with locals and foreigners alike in search of good food and drink. Neon signs throw shifting splinters of color across the streets, giving them a carnival atmosphere. Street vendors fry and boil snacks ranging from squid to hot dogs, all served up on wooden skewers. Shops and restaurants are thrown open to the streets so that you can hear the whack of mahjong tiles, the whir of electric fans, the clink of dishes, and the cheers of locals hoisting glasses of Carlsberg and rice wine with a toast of *Yum sing!*

Rua da Felicidade has become known for specialty meat and sausage shops with names like the Pastelaria Koi Kei and Generos Alimenticios Fong

Seng. Their glass display counters, with their stainless steel trays of pressed meat, dried beef and pork, and links of sausage, entice passersby to purchase traditional Chinese sausage, Portuguese *linguica*, and meats that blend the two into traditional Macanese delicacies. Don't be afraid to ask for a free sample before you buy—the women behind the counters will gladly cut you a morsel of meat with heavy-duty scissors.

You can also watch women make Macanese cookies in their little family-run bakeries that still use traditional charcoal-burning ovens. You will be lured inside by their tempting bakery smell and the chance for some free samples. These lightly sweet cookies are best warm and have a fine, almost sandy texture to them. Almond cookies with Chinese characters stamped on the top are the most well known, though peanut-flavored cookies and sesame-seed cookies are also popular. All are delicious and best enjoyed, say many locals, with a cup of Oolong tea.

You will be hard pressed to know what to drink with the exotic specimens on display in the window tanks of seafood restaurants on Rua da Felicidade. Even if the live snakes, frogs, eels, and various kinds of fish don't appeal to you, they still add a slightly surreal atmosphere to the street.

Like just about everything in old Macau, Rua da Felicidade is actually quite small. Once you've walked its length, branch off into the nearby side streets and continue to explore. You never know what you will find, but you are sure to find something of interest. You won't need to worry about crime, as the area is well policed and safe. No need to worry about getting back to Hong Kong either, since the ferries run all night. Simply pick the most intriguing street and go.

THE BARRIER GATE

Visit the northernmost extreme of the peninsula for a glimpse of mainland China.

Back in the days when China remained largely off limits to foreign travelers, a visit to Macau's border gave you the chance to peer across the frontier at what was then one of the world's most reclusive and mysterious countries. Visitors to Macau peeked through the Bamboo Curtain at the Barrier Gate (Portas do Cerco), located on the narrow spit of land that for nearly 500 years marked the crossing point between Macau and mainland China.

JARDIM DE SAO FRANCISCO

These days China has opened up to the world, so the Barrier Gate no longer draws many foreigners hoping for a look at China. However, the border crossing is now extremely busy, as thousands of Macau residents and mainland Chinese cross back and forth each day, along with a smattering of foreign travelers.

If your plans do not involve a trip to mainland China, but you would still like to catch a glimpse of the world's most populous country, then by all means make a visit to the Portas do Cerco. The name actually translates as "Gates of Siege," which tells you something about the Portuguese state of mind in Macau. There isn't a whole lot to see here of historic value beyond the whitewashed nineteenth-century archway that used to be the official crossing point before the government built modern customs and immigration buildings. In colonial days you could take great photos of the archway with its Portuguese flag, which framed a building across the border waving the Chinese flag. *(Open daily 7 a.m. to midnight. Admission free.)*

These days you will find better photo opportunities in the adjacent **Sun Yat-Sen Park**, one of the larger green spaces on the peninsula. From here you can try to spot the guard posts along the border while photographing the city of Zhuhai across the narrow Duck Channel—

dividing line between Macau and mainland China. You can also explore the park's other features, which include an aviary, a café, a circular greenhouse with foot-massage path, a *feng shui* grove of trees said to bring good luck, and a distinctive footbridge that swirls crazily over a lotus pond. Cross this bridge and you will shake off any pursuing evil spirits, who can only travel in straight lines. *(Open daily 6 a.m. to 11 p.m. Admission free.)*

The Barrier Gate does not fall within realistic walking range of Senate Square, though the determined walker could easily reach it. Nonetheless your best bet is to take a taxi or bus.

JARDIM DE SAO FRANCISCO (GARDEN OF ST. FRANCIS)

Take a time out in a park where pastel pink is the dominant motif.

Pink remains the dominant color of this pleasant, tree-shaded park. The columns and arcades of its ornate fountain are painted a Mediterranean pastel pink with white highlights. With impeccable color coordination, the curious cylindrical building that serves as the park's monument to

World War I has also been painted pink. So too have the railings of the park's central stone staircase. The adjacent Military Club and complex of colonial-era government buildings are likewise—you guessed it—painted in a pink-and-white color scheme. All that pink colonial architecture and subtropical greenery lends the park a quaintly Eurasian atmosphere that borders on quirky—after all, the park also features a pint-sized octagonal library and reading room that looks like a giant Chinese lantern. And if you have never seen an authentic cork tree, then this is definitely the park for you. The gardens can be found at the intersection of Avenida da Praia Grande and Avenida de D. Joao IV, which is just a 15-minute walk from Senate Square. *(See map on pg. 72.)*

THE MACAU TOWER

Head up to the 61st floor for an eagle-eye view of Macau.

There is no escaping the Macau Tower, which looms over the enclave like some kind of sci-fi monster. Many foreign visitors shudder with horror at the sight of the tower, or sputter indignantly about how it has wrecked the city's character. It is hard to argue otherwise, since the Macau Tower sticks out like the proverbial sore thumb. In a city known for its compact and very human scale, the tower is an ungainly and aggressive intruder that just does not fit in. No doubt it suffers from abysmal *feng shui* as well. Some might even say that building the tower was a colossal act of hubris by a city seeking world-class status but unlikely to attain it.

Foreigners complaining about the tower would do well to remember that it was designed by a New Zealand firm, not a Chinese one, so there is plenty of blame to go around in terms of aesthetics. The blame for the original decision to build the tower, however, rests firmly on the shoulders of the powers that be in Macau. That said, my own feeling is that grousing about the city's tallest building serves no useful purpose. The tower is not

THE MACAU TOWER

Good fortune charms for sale near the A–Ma Temple.

The pavilion on the Little Taipa Trail offers panoramic views of the Sai Van Bridge and Macau Tower.

going anywhere, after all, and is there to stay. So I figure, if you can't beat it, join it. Or at least take a ride to the 61st floor for a fantastic view.

At 1,110 feet (339 m), the Macau Tower currently ranks itself as the tenth tallest freestanding tower in the world, though other sources place it a bit lower down on the list. Such quibbling over relative heights hardly matters in terms of the view. After all, on clear days—and China's ever-increasing smokestacks ensure that there aren't many of those—you can see all the way to Hong Kong from the observation deck. The views of Macau itself are always magnificent. In fact, starting your trip to Macau with a visit to the tower's observation deck might not be a bad idea, as it will give you a chance to take in the lay of the land. Armed with this newfound knowledge, you will be far less likely to get lost once back down in the city streets. *(Observation deck open daily 10 a.m. to 9 p.m. Admission MOP$70 for adults and MOP$35 for children.)*

Thrill-seeking in Macau has traditionally been for gamblers, a situation the Macau Tower has been trying to change with its array of imaginative high-altitude activities. You can scale all 1,110 feet of the tower, for example, by climbing the open ladder bolted to the side of the radio mast. You can also bungee jump from 230 feet (70 m) or climb around

the sides of the observation deck without handrails. Though you will be tethered to a safety line at all times, some might nonetheless argue that the Macau Tower is simply offering you another way to gamble.

The Macau Tower is part of the Convention and Entertainment Center, one of the city's post-handover showpieces. Aside from the 60th-floor revolving restaurant, there are more restaurants and cafés on the ground floors, including some grouped around a large outdoor plaza. The complex includes an upscale shopping mall, a mini-theme park for children, a theatre, and a large exhibition area. You can also stroll the promenade along the seawall for a view of the Outer Harbor, the bridges to Taipa, and the irregular bulk of Taipa Island itself.

You can walk to the Macau Tower from Senate Square if you are looking for a little exercise. Just head down Avenida de Almeida Ribeiro and take a right on Avenida da Praia Grande. You will be able to see the tower at this point, so no further directions are necessary. Alternatively, catch a bus or taxi. *(See map on pg. 63.)*

For more details on the Macau Tower, visit the official website at **www.macautower.com.mo.**

❖   ❖   ❖

THE MACAU TOWER

Navigating in Portuguese

Knowing a few key words of the colonial tongue can help you decipher addresses and street names, which are generally given in Portuguese and Chinese, but not English. Here are some useful words for map-reading in Macau:

Alameda: Avenue or boulevard

Alto: Hill

Avenida: Avenue

Beco: Alley

Cais: Dock or wharf

Calcada: Steep street or lane

Caminho: Road or way

Circuito: Exercise circuit or walking trail

Edificio: Building

Estrada: Road or street

Ilha: Island

Istmo: Causeway

Jardim: Garden

Largo: Square or plaza

Mercado: Market

Mirante: Pavilion and lookout point

Monte: Hill

Patio: Small plaza, courtyard, or open area

Ponte: Bridge; also dock or wharf

Praca: Square or plaza

Praia: Beach

Rampa: Steep and often short street

Rotunda: Traffic circle

Rua: Road or street

Travessa: Alley or lane

Trilho: Trail

Vila: Village

Flowers and Swords Greet Morning in Macau

Like many Asian cities, Macau is at its best in the early morning. In the hours bracketing dawn the air feels both cleaner and cooler. Sunlight slants low across the streets, bringing out the vivid colors of the city—the red of the A-Ma Temple, the yellow of St. Dominic's Church, the gold of the goddess Kun Iam statue along the waterfront. The pace of life—never all that fast in Macau—moves along at a pleasant pedestrian speed. Shutters mask the shopfronts and few vehicles cruise the streets. Even the 24-hour casinos are relatively subdued. This is Macau's golden hour, and as those who know the city well will tell you, there is no better time of day to wander its narrow cobbled streets and ornately tiled plazas. If any city warrants setting your alarm clock for an early morning stroll, Macau is surely it.

At the dock-front border post down on Rua do Almirante Sergio the immigration officers stifle yawns as they hear the putt-putt of outboard motors breaking the dawn quiet. They watch as a steady stream of small sampans cruise across the Inner Harbor from China. As is true of so much in Macau—the roads, the cars—the sampans look miniaturized, with frisbee-sized rubber tires dangling from the sides to protect their hulls. The sampans dodge the fishing boats anchored in the harbor and pull up to the floating wharves of the border post.

Up to a half-dozen mainland Chinese jump from each of the tiny square-hulled sampans to the dock. Each passenger will have paid three patacas for the river-taxi crossing. Many carry market goods or work uniforms in plastic bags, and though heavily loaded, move dexterously from the sampan to the wharf. Nobody falls into the water, which is choked with scraps of styrofoam, clumps of uprooted river weed, and other flotsam floating on the tide.

As they do every morning at seven a.m., several larger vessels chug across the river loaded with fresh-cut flowers. These square-bowed ships resemble landing craft, and

when they dock an invading army of women flows down the gangplanks to the wharves. Except for the boat crewmen and the immigration police, there are no men in evidence. Every woman carries a shoulder-pole that resembles a weighing scale. Baskets filled with fresh-cut flowers hang from each end of the scale, their weight evenly balanced. This mass unloading proceeds rapidly and with little hindrance from the police, who give the women's travel documents only the most cursory examination. By 7:45 the ships have returned to China and the women have cleared the open-air customs and immigration building. On the street outside the women load their flowers up on blue flatbed trucks and head off to markets throughout the city.

Not everyone in Macau has gone to work yet, however. A morning *tai chi* session has begun over at the plaza on the corner of Rua de Malaca and Rua de Luis Gonzaga Gomes. The concrete rectangle sits beneath the city's Guia Hill lighthouse, which watches over the *tai chi* practitioners like a protective guardian. *Sifu* (meaning "master") Ping Sau Ling wears a pink silk tunic and pants, and though in her fifties, leads her students with a supple grace. The master's early morning lessons are free and open to anyone interested in learning. She begins with the *tai chi sin* fan dance,

FLOWERS AND SWORDS GREET MORNING IN MACAU

a series of graceful movements that she punctuates by snapping open a large rice-paper fan. Next she wields a sword in a ritualized *tai chi* duel with a fellow master, a routine that is more dance than fight. Both masters swing and swirl their large silver swords in stylized slow-motion arcs, and the rising sun flashes bright white off the blades.

At 8:30 the master and her disciples head off for work on their motorbikes. Many will stop on the way for breakfast, as is true of most everyone in Macau. This is a city fond of good food and drink, after all, and breakfast is no exception. On the narrow lanes leading from Senado Square the city's Portuguese community meets for breakfast at cafés such as U Barril. There they share the latest news over Portuguese coffee, pastries, and sandwiches. Meanwhile Cantonese school kids and adults with Western tastes stop in at one of the McDonald's stationed strategically throughout the city.

The more traditionally minded locals stop in at the Long Wa Teahouse, located on the second floor of a nondescript building opposite the Red Market on Avenida do Almirante Lacerda. Reminiscent of old China, the Long Wa has tiled floors, wooden booths, and cracked white teacups and pots. Ceiling fans whirl overhead, since air-conditioning has never been installed. The almost

exclusively male clientele sips tea, reads newspapers, and converses in high-decibel Cantonese. Some men have brought their brightly colored songbirds in ornate wooden cages, and their warbling calls compete with the swelling traffic noise coming through the open windows like an unwelcome guest. Bonsai plants adorn the balcony of the Long Wa, which offers a view of the flower stalls outside the Red Market. There the women who came over from China that morning sell their flowers to morning shoppers.

By midday many of the flowers are sold and the magic of the morning hours lost to the searing heat of noon and the acrid tang of traffic fumes. Overhead the sun burns the sky white. By 2 p.m. the Long Wa has served lunch and closed for the day; McDonald's has stopped serving its breakfast menu. If business has been good, the flower-market women begin packing up for an early return to their homes in China. Their empty shoulder-baskets swing lightly as kites in the wind, though in just twelve hours they will be laden with another predawn cargo of flowers. Meanwhile, in offices, shops, and kitchens around the city *tai chi* students eagerly look forward to the next morning, Macau's most magic hour.

Fresh flowers surround a vendor near Senate Square.

FLOWERS AND SWORDS GREET MORNING IN MACAU

A City of Bridges

Three white bridges bind Macau together, but these graceful spans may soon be dwarfed
by an 18-mile-long super bridge linking Macau to Hong Kong.

Like many cities around the world from London to Leningrad, Macau is a city of bridges. Three graceful white bridges keep the islands of Taipa and Coloane firmly tethered to peninsular Macau. A fourth bridge on the COTAI Strip links Taipa and Coloane to the mainland.

Bridges are a relatively new development in Macau, as the first bridge to Taipa Island only opened in 1974. Like so many things in Macau, this bridge has multiple names that reflect the enclave's multilingual heritage. The colonial government gave it an official Portuguese name—Ponte Governador Nobre de Carvalho. English-speakers refer to it as the Macau-Taipa Bridge, while the local Cantonese came to call it the Old Bridge.

The Macau-Taipa Bridge begins at the roundabout by the gaudy Lisboa Hotel before crossing the channel to Taipa, with an arched portion midway across to leave room for ships to pass beneath. The 1.5-mile-long (2.5 km) bridge only has two lanes, but nonetheless opened the traditionally rural Taipa and Coloane up to modern development.

The nearly three-mile-long (4.5 km) Friendship Bridge—Ponte da Amizade—opened in 1994. This four-lane span is longer and wider than the Macau-Taipa Bridge, but follows a similar design. The two long white bridges complemented each other like a pair of siblings. Like the first bridge, the Friendship Bridge also fueled the development of Taipa and Coloane.

The alleviation of rush-hour traffic jams remained one of the official reasons for the construction of the new Sai Van Bridge— the third bridge to Taipa. Other unofficial factors may have carried more weight—principally that the various companies involved in building the bridge would make a nice profit, and, in the process, boost a lackluster local economy, reduce unemployment, and thereby increase the popularity of the local government. More broadly, the bridge continued to feed Macau's

Lead photo description on page 191

appetite for large-scale public works projects of suspect value. Macau's international airport, for example, opened in 1995 but as predicted immediately suffered from competition with airports in Zhuhai, Shenzhen, Guangzhou, and Hong Kong. Some say the airport should never have been built, though its recent success as a budget airline hub may yet prove the skeptics wrong.

Construction crews completed the Sai Van Bridge in December 2004, just in time for the fifth anniversary celebrations of Macau's return to China. The 1.4-mile-long (2.2 km) bridge opened to traffic in early 2005. Unlike the other two bridges to Taipa, the Sai Van Bridge has two decks. The enclosed lower deck will allow it to remain open during typhoons, which periodically sweep across Macau from May to November. In the past, residents of Taipa and Coloane had been marooned during typhoons, that forced the closure of the open-deck Macau-Taipa and Friendship bridges.

Ultimately, however, the Sai Van Bridge's enclosed lower deck will carry a portion of the city's light-rail system. If all goes as planned, by 2009 the first line will run down the Macau peninsula and over the Sai Van Bridge to end on Taipa. A later spur line will serve the airport. A third line will circle the Macau peninsula with a string of metro stops. The light-rail system is just the latest of many ambitious public works projects that have reshaped the face of Macau, often for the worse. Fortunately, the light-rail system will generally run underground so its impact on the city's character will be minimized. Getting around the city will certainly be easier, and road congestion might ease a bit, too—but whether the system will earn the revenue needed to justify its huge price tag remains an open question.

Meanwhile, Beijing has given the green light to one of the world's largest construction projects—an eighteen-mile-long (29 km) highway bridge linking Hong Kong, Macau, and the mainland city of Zhuhai just across the enclave's border with China. Dubbed the "super bridge" by the media, it promises to be an engineering marvel of the sort only Hong Kong can produce. Despite its astounding length, however, it will not be the world's longest bridge—that honor goes to the 24-mile-long (38.5 km) Second Lake Pontchartrain Causeway in Louisiana.

The super bridge will still be plenty long, however, as well as very expensive. The estimated US$4 billion price tag will be covered primarily by the private sector. Budget overruns seem likely, however, as the estimated costs have been rising steadily since its backers first proposed the project. Hong Kong and Beijing will invest considerable capital and prestige in the super bridge, so once construction crews start driving the first pilings, it will take much more than rising cost estimates to shut the project down. As of mid-2006 construction had not yet begun on the super bridge, however, and start dates for the project continue to be pushed forward.

Current plans call for the bridge to begin at Hong Kong's international airport on Lantau Island, which is already connected to the rest of the city by the impressive Tsing Ma highway bridge. From Lantau the super bridge will cross the Pearl River Delta, then make a Y-shaped split into two branches—one to Macau and one to Zhuhai. To accommodate the large number of ships in the Pearl River Delta, the bridge will change to a tunnel that runs between a pair of artificial islands built mid-channel.

If all goes as planned, the much-debated route of the super bridge will preserve Hong Kong's dominant position as the financial and logistics hub of the Pearl River Delta—and scupper the ambitions of western Guangdong Province to overtake Hong Kong and become the chief transshipment point for the region's exports. For this reason, the powerbrokers of Guangdong Province have been less than enthused about the super bridge, but have apparently consoled themselves with the recognition that it will nonetheless spur overall economic development throughout the Pearl River Delta. They have also proposed a new high-speed rail line that could compete with the super bridge by carrying cargo to container terminals in Guangdong Province—cargo that would otherwise be trucked via the bridge to terminals in Hong Kong.

Though it will benefit Hong Kong most of all, the super bridge will hasten the more general economic integration of the cities in the Pearl River Delta and likely benefit all of them, including Macau. Hong Kong's gamblers will be able to shorten their travel time to Macau by taking buses instead of ferries. They could even drive their own cars, though building parking garages in Macau for all those autos will be just one of the many spin-off challenges from this massive bridge project. Macau's shoppers and weekenders, meanwhile, will be able to more easily hit the malls in Kowloon as well as jack up ticket sales at the newly opened Hong Kong Disneyland.

The super bridge will not bring entirely positive results, however. Environmental activists fear the bridge's construction will further threaten the endangered dolphins of the Pearl River Delta as well as destroy green space on Lantau Island, one of Hong Kong's most beautiful undeveloped areas. The backers of Guangdong Province's new container terminal fear their project will be unable to compete with Hong Kong's already dominant cargo terminal, even with the new high-speed rail line. Companies involved with moving freight by sea between the delta's various cities fear a loss of business, as trucks will be able to haul cargo over the super bridge.

The ferry companies will certainly suffer, as travel times from Hong Kong to Macau, now about 60 minutes by jetfoil, will be reduced to half that by bus. While the Hong Kong-Macau jetfoils won't disappear, they may have to scale back their service and lower their fares to remain competitive as passenger numbers fall. However, a robust demand for the ferries will likely remain. Tourists will continue to take the ferries for the scenic ride, and many Hong Kong and Macau residents live close enough to the ferry terminals to make a jetfoil as convenient as a bus across the super bridge. What's more, the ferries are more comfortable than even the most luxurious buses, rough weather days excepted.

Despite the downsides, few doubt that it will be good for Macau to have the super bridge. Certainly it will be fitting. After all, Macau has long been a city of bridges, so why not give it what so few cities of the world can boast—the ultimate super bridge, backed by four other bridges of unusual length and aesthetic beauty.

Ultimately, these bridges serve as a metaphor for Macau itself. The tiny enclave has long been a bridge between China and the outside world. Macau has bridged the centuries as well, so that you can find a Starbucks and a sixteenth-century Catholic church on the same square. Most of all, Macau has bridged two cultures, linking the Portuguese and the Cantonese in a cross-cultural fusion. In this sense, Macau has truly built one of the world's most unique bridges.

❖ ❖ ❖

Typhoon!

Only a severe typhoon can shut down Macau's casinos. When one of these monster storms roars in from the South China Sea, the city performs the municipal equivalent of curling into a fetal ball and closing its eyes. The storm warning flags go up the mast beside the Guia Hill lighthouse. Schools, businesses, and government offices close. Workers tape the city's windows and apartment dwellers clear their balconies of anything that might blow away. Boats head for the sanctuary of the Inner Harbor. Two of the three bridges out to Taipa are closed to traffic, with only the new Sai Van Bridge's typhoon-proof lower deck remaining open. If the typhoon becomes severe enough, even the casinos have to shut down.

The word "typhoon" derives from the Cantonese tai fung, which translates as "big wind." Typhoons certainly qualify as big winds, with top gusts reaching 160 mph (260 kph). Sometimes called tropical cyclones, typhoons are given names drawn from a pool of names submitted by various Asian nations. They strike Macau between May and November, with August and September the peak months. In Macau, typhoons often drop massive amounts of rain. According to the Macau Meteorological and Geophysical Bureau, in the last few decades typhoons have also produced sustained winds of up to 77 mph (124 kph) and peak gusts of up to 112 mph (181 kph).

Typhoons are closely monitored by the Meteorological and Geophysical Bureau (also known by its Portuguese acronym of SMG), which maintains an efficient alert system consisting of different typhoon warning signals. The scale starts with typhoon warning #1 (symbolized by a "T"), which indicates a typhoon is within 500 miles (800 km) of the city. Somewhat eccentrically, there is no #2 warning, so the next threat level is typhoon warning #3 (symbolized by an upside down "T"). A #3 warning indicates a typhoon is approaching Macau and that wind gusts have already risen to 40 mph (62 kph) in the city. The system then leaps ahead to typhoon warning #8 (symbolized by a triangle), which indicates a typhoon has arrived with winds of 40 to 70 mph (63 to 117 kph). Though warning signals #9 and #10 exist, they are rarely hoisted as they indicate an unusually powerful storm. In other words, while a storm that triggers typhoon warning #8 will cancel work and school for the day, a storm worthy of a #9 or #10 signal will blow the office or school right into the harbor.

If you are a storm lover like me, you will find riding out a typhoon in Macau to be the high point of your trip. After all, you will be safely on land, not out at sea. For those who see giant meteorological events like typhoons as nothing more than a wet and windy inconvenience, rest assured that the odds are against your visit to Macau coinciding with a visit from a typhoon.

To keep track of the weather in Macau, all you have to do is dial 1311. Press extension 4 and you will get an English-language weather report from the SMG, complete with typhoon warnings. Alternatively, visit the SMG website at **www. smg.gov.mo**. The *South China Morning Post*, the Hong Kong newspaper that serves as Macau's de-facto English-language paper, also provides detailed daily weather reports.

A bus crosses the Macau-Taipa Bridge, while the Sai Van Bridge rises in the background.

Traffic flows across the Macau-Taipa Bridge.

A City of Bridges

Taipa Island: Macau's Suburb

Taipa offers a classic Macanese blend of ultramodern high-rises and timeworn village lanes, spiced with green hillsides, colonial villas, traditional temples, and plenty of places to eat.

While the Portuguese first settled on the Macau peninsula in 1557, the islands of Taipa and Coloane did not come under their control until the mid-1800s. At this time the Ching dynasty had just been defeated by the British during the Opium War, leaving China wide open to Western exploitation. When the British took Hong Kong from a prostrate China in 1842, the Portuguese grabbed the chance to acquire some new real estate as well. Starting in 1847, the colonial administration began taking control of three islands located off the tip of the Macau peninsula—Taipa Grande, Taipa Pequena, and Kun Iam. In 1864, the Portuguese also claimed the much larger Coloane. The Portuguese wanted these four islands primarily because they offered a protected anchorage deeper than the shallow Inner Harbor on the Macau peninsula, allowing larger vessels to drop anchor that might have otherwise had to bypass the colony altogether. The Portuguese backed up their newly asserted authority over the islands by building a fortified garrison on the western side of Taipa Pequena that came to be known as Taipa Fort.

Ironically, the small Chinese communities on the islands volunteered the funds to pay for Taipa Fort, as they wanted the Portuguese navy to protect them from the pirates that cruised the surrounding waters like hungry sharks. That their villages would be absorbed into a European colony in the process did not unduly concern the local Chinese, who like islanders everywhere looked primarily to the sea for their livelihoods. In that sense, they had much in common with the Portuguese. Most of the islanders made an honest living from fishing, ferrying, and junk building. A smaller number, however, relied on smuggling and piracy, giving the islands a reputation for lawlessness that persisted into the twentieth century. The islands remained a pirate haven until as late as 1910, in fact, when the Portuguese authorities finally rounded up the last of the buccaneers on Coloane Island.

Lead photo description on page 191

Taipa and Coloane could only be reached by boat until the 1970s, which preserved the traditional character of the islands and left them relatively undeveloped. Ferries like the *Hoi Tak* steamed between Taipa and peninsular Macau until 1974, when the Macau-Taipa Bridge finally linked the island to the urban Macau peninsula. The Friendship Bridge opened 20 years later, further connecting Taipa to the city center. The opening of the typhoon-proof Sai Van Bridge in early 2005 meant that for all practical purposes Taipa no longer qualified as an island. The all-weather bridge ensured guaranteed access to peninsular Macau, thereby accelerating the ongoing integration of Taipa with the enclave's highly urbanized city center.

Along with the bridges, large-scale land-reclamation projects also brought the modern world to the islands. Some of the most ambitious land-reclamation schemes focused on Taipa, which in the past few decades has grown like a young lily pad on a lotus pond. In 2004 the Macau Cartography and Cadastre Bureau pegged Taipa's landmass at about 2.5 square miles (6.4 sq. km), though by now additional land reclamation will have rendered that statistic as out of date as a quote from a year-old stock report. The original three islands of Taipa Grande, Taipa Pequena, and Kun Iam have been joined together so seamlessly that a visitor would never know that modern-day Taipa once consisted of three separate islets.

A visitor might also have to make a special effort to see that Taipa once consisted of little more than a few traditional villages on an otherwise rural island. Vestiges of this lost era do remain, however. Contemporary Taipa, in fact, remains a mix of old and new, where high-rise apartment blocks overlook colonial buildings and traditional Chinese temples, some dating as far back as the late 1600s.

This juxtaposition of old and new corresponds with an even more startling contrast between large and small. In some ways,

Taipa is strictly small scale. After all, size-wise the island borders on the lilliputian, and its residents only number about 42,000 people—just 10% of Macau's total population. Taipa Village, the traditional heart of the island, is a compact warren of narrow lanes and alleyways lined by shops and homes rarely more than three stories tall. But if traditional equals small on Taipa, then modern equals large. In fact, everything new on Taipa tends to be massive in size. The international airport, for example, features an offshore runway longer than the island itself. This 11,021-foot landing strip (3,360 m) resembles a gigantic concrete aircraft carrier, with airliners whizzing aloft like scrambling fighter jets. Taipa also hosts a horse track at the Macau Jockey Club, several major hotels and casinos, the University of Macau, and a small forest of apartment blocks reminiscent of Hong Kong's so-called New Towns. Long considered Macau's suburb, the island will soon evolve into a full-fledged satellite city.

That said, Taipa still maintains, if just barely, a balance between the wired-up 24/7 demands of city life and the sleepy torpor of village life. On Taipa you can hear the jingle of mobile phones and rumble of rising airliners—but you can also hear the clang of church bells, the whack of mahjong tiles, the call of caged songbirds, and all the other age-old sounds of traditional village life. More broadly, you could say that the whole island remains a village set apart from the big city of peninsular Macau. Taipa feels more laidback than downtown Macau, and though this slow-paced atmosphere gets ratcheted up a notch with each new apartment block built on the island, life still proceeds at a less frenetic pace.

This more relaxed pace can be attributed not just to Taipa's village heritage, but also to its abundance of green space. The forested ridges of the original three islands still dominate Taipa, and their overgrown heights give a liberating feeling of natural open space so lacking on the jam-packed Macau peninsula. Their impact on the atmosphere of the island cannot be overstated—those shaggy ridges, above all else, make Taipa distinct from paved-over peninsular Macau. From the Macau peninsula you can see these peaks when you stroll along the edge of the Outer Harbor, when you stand atop Penha Hill, and when you ride the elevator up the Macau Tower. The enticing outline of those distant green hills, in fact, will most likely be what draws you over the bridge to Taipa in the first place.

Like most foreign visitors, you probably have a limited amount of time to spend in Macau—perhaps just a single day. However, you don't have to let this rule out a sortie to the islands. After all, Macau's small size and trio of bridges ensures that you can easily reach Taipa Village—center point of most visits to the island—in as little as ten minutes by taxi. Assuming you have a relatively small amount of time to play with, I suggest that you limit your visit to Taipa Village and the adjacent Taipa House Museum—an excursion described below in the Taipa Village Walk.

However, for those visitors with a little more time to spend on Taipa, I have described two additional walking routes that when combined with the Taipa Village Walk take in virtually all the sites that the island has to offer. Ambitious walkers can string all three routes together and easily cover them in a day's time, with an hour or two to spare for a long Macanese lunch lubricated with a carafe of *vinho verde*.

If you have a little extra cash and/or can split the fare among several passengers, take a taxi out to Taipa from the Macau peninsula. Fares are around MOP$35 to Taipa Village, so the price is right. After all, taxis are quicker and simpler than the buses, which can be crowded to the point that you can't get a seat. That said, bus service is reasonably frequent and certainly affordable. You can catch a bus to Taipa on Avenida de Almeida Ribeiro; alternatively, many buses to the island stop in front of the Lisboa

Hotel. Buses 11, 22, 28A, 33, 34, and AP1 all run to Taipa (MOP$3.3). Buses 21, 21A, 25, and 26A also go to Taipa, but continue on to Coloane as well—hence the higher fare of MOP$4 or 5. Bus 15 runs just between Taipa and Coloane (MOP$2.8).

While all three bridges to Taipa offer memorable views, I recommend that you take the recently renovated Macau-Taipa Bridge if you can. Crossing this narrow two-lane span always reminds me of a short airline flight, minus the security checks. After circling the roundabout outside the Lisboa Hotel, you turn onto the bridge and skim low over the waters on a runway-like stretch that is more causeway than bridge span. On your left you can see the silt-brown waters over a low guardrail; on your right oncoming traffic whizzes past with just a few feet to spare. Straight ahead the hills of Taipa rise before you like anticipation itself. Suddenly you climb steeply into the air where the bridge arches gracefully in mid-channel. You can see tugs, barges, fishing boats, and small freighters trailing white wakes in the channel below. Then you swoop back down the opposite side of the arch, continue along another stretch of low bridge, and land on Taipa's northern shore. Just like you do with an airline flight, you reach an entirely new place that is unlike the one you left, for Taipa is distinctly different from peninsular Macau.

TAIPA VILLAGE WALK

With its colonial villas and narrow lanes lined with open-air restaurants, Taipa village remains the highlight of any visit to the island.

This walk starts at the Taipa House Museum on Avenida da Praia. Taxis can drop you directly at the museum, while buses can drop you on Rua Direita Carlos Eugenio, which is almost as close. From the bus stop, climb the stairs of the Calcada do Carmo to the plaza outside Our Lady of Carmo Church, then take the cobblestone ramp down the other side to the pastel-green villas of the Taipa House Museum. Keep in mind that the diminutive scale of Taipa Village means that any bus stop will be just a short walk from the museum, so alighting at the stop on Carlos Eugenio isn't critically important.

The Taipa House Museum

The Taipa House Museum has become a symbol of the city nearly as famous as the ruins of St. Paul's Church or the Guia Hill lighthouse— and rightfully so, as here you will find an attractive cobblestone promenade fronted by five lovingly restored colonial villas standing in the shade of venerable banyan trees. Built in 1921, these green-and-white villas housed Portuguese and Macanese colonial officials back in the days when Taipa could only be reached by ferry. The stucco villas mix European and Chinese architecture, with deep verandahs and louvered window shutters. Most visitors will feel like they have just stepped into a movie set, though the villas, banyans, and cobblestones are completely authentic.

This movie-set atmosphere only intensifies when you enter the most interesting of the five villas, which displays a mix of Portuguese and Cantonese furniture, utensils, paintings, and décor typical for the Macanese families that once lived in these houses, complete with family altar, statuettes of Catholic saints, and silk painting of the goddess Kun Iam.

Of the remaining four villas, one contains displays devoted to life in Portugal, another describes the history of Taipa and Coloane, and a third houses temporary exhibits. Receptions and other official events take place in the last villa. Collectively the five villas and their grounds are known as the Taipa House Museum. A European-style kiosk offers cold drinks and snacks, making the museum's cobblestone boulevard a pleasant spot to take a rest. Have a seat on a shaded wrought-iron park

Taipa Village Walk

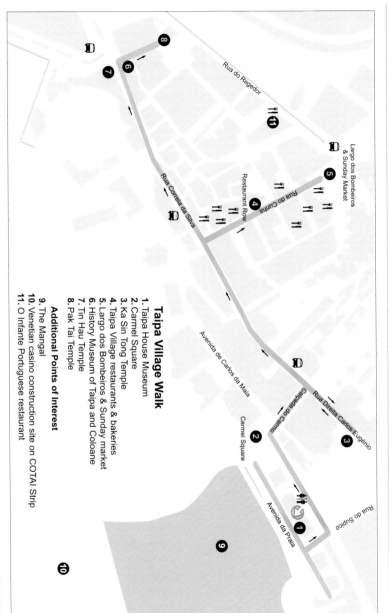

Taipa Village Walk
1. Taipa House Museum
2. Carmel Square
3. Ka Sin Tong Temple
4. Taipa Village restaurants & bakeries
5. Largo dos Bombeiros & Sunday market
6. History Museum of Taipa and Coloane
7. Tin Hau Temple
8. Pak Tai Temple

Additional Points of Interest
9. The Mangal
10. Venetian casino construction site on COTAI Strip
11. O Infante Portuguese restaurant

bench and soak up the atmosphere of old Macau.

Unfortunately, the boulevard's seaside view has disappeared. The Avenida da Praia, which literally translates as Beach Avenue, once fronted a sandy strip along the channel running between Taipa and Coloane islands. This convenient location provided sea breezes and easy access to the ships that anchored in the protected channel offshore. Today's view is considerably less romantic, as the channel has been completely filled in to create the COTAI Strip gambling district dominated by the massive Venetian casino complex. Fortunately, however, **the Mangal** offers a buffer zone between the Taipa House Museum and the COTAI Strip. This small lake with a marshy shoreline has been preserved as the enclave's only wetland, though its future remains very much in doubt. Here you can see plenty of the lotus flowers so beloved in Macau and featured on its flag, as well as a surprisingly large array of birdlife. *(Grounds open 24/7. Displays inside villas open 10 a.m. to 6 p.m. Closed Mondays. Admission to villas MOP$5.)*

Carmel Square (Largo do Carmo)

Walk up the cobblestone ramp behind the Taipa House Museum to the Largo do Carmo, a small plaza fronted by Our Lady of Carmel Church and the Taipa Library.

Built on a low rise in 1885, Our Lady of Carmel holds the dual distinction of being the island's first as well as the island's only Catholic church. When the hilltop church held its first mass some 120 years ago, its 35 parishioners could see both the Taipa-Coloane Channel and the Macau peninsula. A stone cross still marks this lookout point on the church plaza, though these days the channel has been filled in and the peninsula hidden behind a thicket of high-rises.

The Taipa Library stands across the square in a graceful counterpoint to the church. Though you would never know it, the beige-colored library with its white colonnades is actually a reproduction of the original *biblioteca* that stood on this site. The light-yellow building to the left of the library is an original structure, however, constructed in the early 1900s as a school and now used as a center for the elderly. A pleasant public garden can be found behind the library.

Taipa Village

From the Largo do Carmo, walk down the Calcada do Carmo staircase and turn right onto Rua Direita Carlos Eugenio. Walk up this street until you see the hundred-year-old **Ka Sin Tong Temple**, dedicated to Leng, the god of medicine. Not surprisingly, worshippers come to this temple to pray for good health, healing, and happiness. The walls across the street from the temple conceal the grounds of a former fireworks factory. Retrace your steps down Eugenio past the Calcada do Carmo, and turn right on pedestrian-only Rua do Cunha.

Many know Rua do Cunha as Food Street or Restaurant Row. This ruler-straight alleyway will take you into the heart of Taipa Village, which often feels like one gigantic international food court. Open-air restaurants line both sides of Rua do Cunha as well as the adjoining alleys, offering Portuguese, Macanese, Chinese, and a host of other cuisines. *(For suggestions on where to eat, see pg. 147.)*

Take any alleyway leading off Rua do Cunha and wander through Taipa Village, a small and compact community resting in the shadow of high-rise tower blocks. The village blends European and Chinese architecture with the same abandon that it mixes colors, with doors, shutters, and walls painted a pastel rainbow of yellows, pinks, blues, and greens. Multicolored flags strung across the alleys dangle overhead. Family-run shops sell vegetables, fruit, soft drinks, and Portuguese wine. The village's famous bakeries offer pastries, peanut candy, and Macanese cookies. You never know what each twist in a narrow lane will reveal—perhaps a graceful colonial home, perhaps an old temple, perhaps a pleasant plaza.

If you wish to learn more about the history of Taipa and Coloane, walk over to the recently opened **History Museum of Taipa and Coloane** on Rua Correia da Silva. Appropriately, this museum occupies the former Island Council Building, a colonial edifice painted in the island's trademark pastel green. *(Open 10 a.m. to 6 p.m. Closed Mondays. Admission MOP$5.)*

Across the street from the museum you will find yet another **temple dedicated to Tin Hau**, otherwise known as A-Ma. In this case, the temple dates to 1785, though the current building was built in 1838 with funds provided by local Chinese merchants and fishermen as well as the widows of Chinese militiamen killed in battle with the South China Sea's rapacious pirates.

In the nearby Largo Camoes (Camoes Square) you can visit the ornate **Pak Tai Temple**, which dates to 1844 and is the only temple in Macau dedicated to the Taoist deity Pak Tai, god of the north.

On Sundays from 11 a.m. to 8 p.m., a combination street fair and flea market fills the square outside the Pak Tai Temple as well as the larger Largo dos Bombeiros and the streets in between. Here you can browse stalls selling everything from balloons to antique opium pipes. If you like the excitement of a crowd and hope to find a memorable souvenir at a bargain price, then Sunday is a good time to visit Taipa Village. *(See pg. 164 for more on the Sunday market.)* If you aren't willing to elbow your way down narrow lanes clogged with shoppers, however, then you should come on a quieter weekday.

On to Coloane Island

After exploring Taipa Village, you have two options. If you have sufficient time, you can continue to explore Taipa Island by following the suggested walking routes below. If you have a limited amount of time, however, then you should catch a taxi or bus to Coloane Village on Coloane Island *(see pg. 120)*. You can find a bus stop by crossing Largo dos Bombeiros (Firemen Square, so named for the station that used to front the plaza) at the end of Rua do Cunha. The bus stop is located just across the street from the plaza, on Rua do Regedor. You should also be able to hail a taxi from this location, though keep in mind that if you eat at any restaurant in the village you can ask the staff to call you a taxi.

❖   ❖   ❖

TAIPA GRANDE WALK

Stroll around the green slopes of Taipa Grande Hill, take in some panoramic views, and have a look at a hillside cemetery with some awesome feng shui.

If you are starting this walk in Taipa Village, cross Largo dos Bombeiros at the end of Rua do Cunha and head up Rua da Ponte Negra one block to Avenida Olimpica. Turn right on Olimpica and continue to the *rotunda*—as the Portuguese call traffic circles. On the opposite side of the circle, continue on Estrada Coronel Nicolau de Mesquita. You will soon reach the rather grandiosely named **Lakeside Garden**, which features little more than a small fountain pond. Just before the garden Estrada Padre Estevao Eusebio Situ winds steeply uphill to a parking area where the Grand Taipa Trail begins. This trail does not get much use, which means you can have Taipa Grande pretty much to yourself. This is no small thing in a city with some of the highest population densities in the world. When I last hiked the trail I met just one other person—a friendly forest ranger riding a lime-green

TAIPA GRANDE WALK

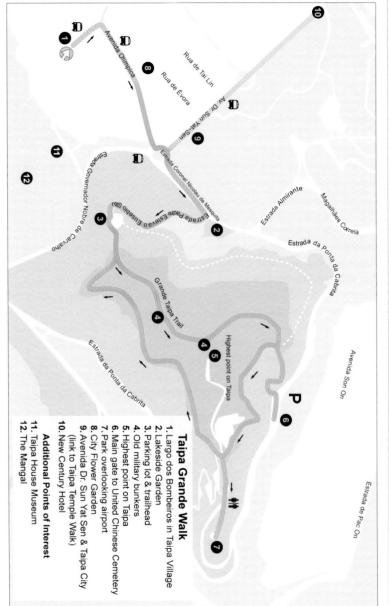

Taipa Grande Walk

1. Largo dos Bombeiros in Taipa Village
2. Lakeside Garden
3. Parking lot & trailhead
4. Old military bunkers
5. Highest point on Taipa
6. Main gate to United Chinese Cemetery
7. Park overlooking airport
8. City Flower Garden
9. Avenida Dr. Sun Yat Sen & Taipa City
   (link to Taipa Temple Walk)
10. New Century Hotel

Additional Points of Interest

11. Taipa House Museum
12. The Mangal

municipal motorbike. *(For more on trail conditions, see "Hiking in Macau" on pg. 136.)*

From the parking area you will have a fantastic view of Taipa Village and the COTAI Strip. The pastel-green houses of the Taipa House Museum will be directly below you. You will also be able to see **the Mangal**, a small lake with some marshy, overgrown shoreline that serves as Macau's only refuge for migratory birds. Despite its small size, however, the Mangal attracts an impressive number of birds. In the distance you will be able to observe construction crews working on the huge concrete skeleton of the Venetian casino complex and the rest of the COTAI Strip. The ongoing bang of pile drivers and rattle of rock-breaking equipment provides an industrial soundtrack. When I visited Macau in spring 2006, I counted over 40 construction cranes of various shapes and sizes working to erect this huge building. By the time you make your visit, the Venetian will probably be open for business. Beyond the shell of the Venetian, you can see the Macau Egg—as locals call the domed East Asian Games stadium—and the green bulk of Coloane Island.

If you do not wish to walk to the trailhead, a taxi can drop you there. Your best bus stop is at the *rotunda* on Avenida Olimpica.

Grand Taipa Trail

From the parking area at the end of Estrada Padre Estevao Eusebio Situ, take the more challenging trail that heads straight uphill in a long series of stone steps. Though you will be walking in the shade, just a few decades ago you would have been scrambling up a boulder-strewn slope devoid of trees. Taipa Grande's forested landscape is a testament to Macau's reforestation efforts and one of its few environmental success stories. You will soon pass several abandoned military bunkers as the path angles steeply uphill to 525 feet (160 m)—the highest point on Taipa. Trees obscure the view from this modest summit, however.

Continue down the path until you reach the main trail. Cross the main trail and continue downhill to Estrada da Ponta da Cabrita. When you reach the street, you will find yourself opposite the walls of the United Chinese Cemetery. You can find the main entrance to the cemetery by turning right and walking about 150 feet (50 m) down the road.

United Chinese Cemetery

No fewer than eight cemeteries dot the slopes of Taipa, which has long served as Macau's graveyard. Like the scattered pages of an old history book, the tombs and gravestones of these burial grounds trace Macau's history. Victims of the

1874 typhoon rest in one cemetery; in another lie those killed in an explosion at a fireworks factory. Fortunately, they won't be joined by any new casualties, as Taipa's last pyrotechnic factory has shut its doors and awaits redevelopment. Many of the enclave's most famous residents have found a permanent home in the cemeteries of Taipa, including Madam Lou Mou Cheng, first wife of Dr. Sun Yat-Sen. But whether they belong to a *taipan* or a peasant, all tombs and graves have been situated according to the rules of *feng shui*, a widely practiced form of Chinese geomancy that translates as "wind and water." Thus the ghosts of Taipa rest easy.

While visiting any graveyard on Taipa can be an interesting experience from a cultural and historical standpoint, I recommend the United Chinese Cemetery above all the others. This cemetery occupies a scenic location on a hillside clearly visible when you cross to Taipa on the Friendship Bridge. Chinese of Buddhist, Taoist, and Confucian faith are buried here in terraced rows of graves cut into the cliffside to face the sea—a crucial requirement for good *feng shui*. A huge statue of Tou Tei, the earth god, stands watch over the cemetery.

When you have finished touring the cemetery, return to the trailhead, walk uphill and bear to the left when you reach the main trail. Continue until you reach the **park that**

overlooks Macau International Airport. From here you will have an excellent view of planes taking off from the two-mile runway (3.3 km) longer than the trail itself. From the observation area, continue around Taipa Grande until you reach your original starting point at the parking area on Estrada Padre Estevao Eusebio Situ.

You can easily link this walk with the Taipa Temple Walk *(see pg. 108)* by returning to the Avenida Olimpica *rotunda*. From there head up Avenida Dr. Sun Yat-Sen, which will give you a chance to stroll through Taipa City, a rather functional neighborhood of high-rise apartment blocks. The **City Flower Garden** on Rua de Evora offers a welcome respite from all that concrete and steel, with its manicured grounds modeled on a classical Chinese garden complete with lotus ponds, winding bridges, pavilions, and plenty of greenery. Stop in for a floral-scented break, then proceed up Avenida Dr. Sun Yat-Sen to the traffic circle by the New Century Hotel, starting point of the Taipa Temple Walk.

TAIPA TEMPLE WALK

On this walk you can pay your respects to Kun Iam, eat vegetarian with the monks, and enjoy some great hilltop views.

This walk begins at the traffic circle by the New Century Hotel on the north side of Taipa, which you can easily reach by taxi or bus from the Macau peninsula.

Kun Iam Temple

Though the Kun Iam Temple is neither the oldest nor the largest place of worship on Taipa, it may well be one of the smallest. This little temple nestles on a rock ledge against the steep slope of Kun Iam Hill. The modernistic buildings of Macau University squat atop the hill and the bulk of the garish New Century Hotel stands nearby, dwarfing the pint-sized temple. This half-forgotten shrine receives few visitors, so chances are you will have the place to yourself.

A wide staircase leads up to the temple, which has an exterior of whitewashed walls with red trim. Smoking incense coils hang from the eaves and two stone lions flank the doors like a pair of ever-vigilant sentries. The interior contains the original rock grotto that local fishermen first used as an impromptu shrine to Kun Iam, the goddess of mercy and general protector of Macau. The fishermen constructed the temple itself at a later date, though lack of funds meant they went for a gong-like slice of metal shaped like a lucky bat rather than a more expensive temple bell.

The temple once stood on the coast of the island, though land-reclamation has now left it stranded a good distance inland. Fortunately, the temple still has a waterfront view, which includes the Macau-Taipa Bridge and Sai Van Bridge as well as the Macau Tower. This view will disappear, however, if a casino or other project is built on the reclaimed land in front of the temple. That would be a pity, for much of the temple's magic lies in its location. The temple backs up against the former coastline, which was a jumble of huge, timeworn boulders. Large banyan trees run huge roots over the boulders and shade the temple. Standing snugly against an overgrown hillside, the temple offers a quiet refuge and a serene sense of moving backwards in time to when just a few fishing families lived on the island.

To reach the temple from the traffic circle, head a short distance up Avenida Padre Tomas Pereira.

TAIPA TEMPLE WALK

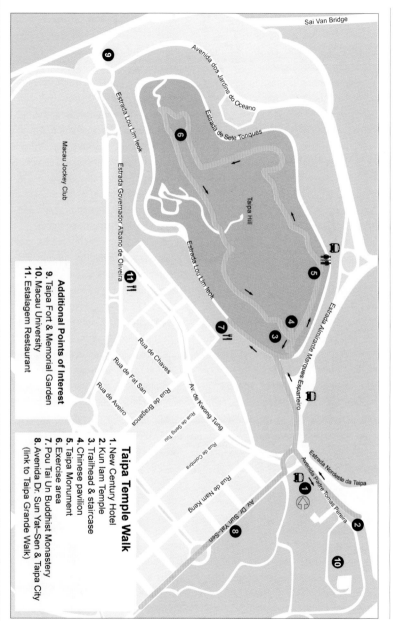

Sai Van Bridge

Avenida dos Jardins do Oceano

Estrada de Sete Tonques

Estrada Lou Lim Ieok

Estrada Governador Albano de Oliveira

Macau Jockey Club

Taipa Hill

Estrada Lou Lim Ieok

Estrada Almirante Marques Esparteiro

Rua de Chaves

Rua de Fat San

Rua de Bragança

Rua de Aveiro

Av. de Kwong Tung

Rua de Seng Tou

Rua de Coimbra

Rua de Nam Keng

Av. Dr. Sun Yat-Sen

Estrada Nordeste da Taipa

Avenida Padre Tomás Pereira

Additional Points of Interest

9. Taipa Fort & Memorial Garden
10. Macau University
11. Estalagem Restaurant

Taipa Temple Walk

1. New Century Hotel
2. Kun Iam Temple
3. Trailhead & staircase
4. Chinese pavilion
5. Taipa Monument
6. Exercise area
7. Pou Tai Un Buddhist Monastery
8. Avenida Dr. Sun Yat-Sen & Taipa City
   (link to Taipa Grande Walk)

The New Century Hotel will be on your right as you walk, and you will soon see a staircase on your left that descends to the temple.

When you have finished paying your respects to Kun Iam, return to the traffic circle by climbing back up the staircase behind the temple.

The Little Taipa Trail and Taipa Monument

The 1.4-mile (2.3 km) Little Taipa Trail circles the upper slopes of Taipa Pequena—once a separate islet, but now just a hill absorbed into the larger landmass of modern-day Taipa. Though this trail is popular with joggers, it is never crowded, so it offers a nice respite from the jam-packed streets of downtown Macau. Little Taipa provides some fine views, plenty of flowering plants, and numerous birds and butterflies. The trail takes about an hour at a meandering pace and hardly ranks as an arduous trek. *(For more on trail conditions, see "Hiking in Macau" on pg. 136.)*

To reach the trail, walk from the traffic circle for a very short distance along Estrada Almirante Marques Esparteiro and then head left up Estrada Lou Lim Ieok. Almost immediately you will need to turn right onto Estrada de Sete Tanques, which angles steeply up Taipa Pequena Hill. A short distance up Sete Tanques you will see the staircase that marks the start of the Little Taipa Trail.

The climb up the initial staircase to the main portion of the trail remains the only truly strenuous part of the hike, so do not let it dissuade you from continuing. Once you have made the five-minute climb, you will intersect the main trail that runs around Taipa Pequena like a gravel halo. You will also see a Chinese pavilion, which you can reach by climbing another hundred steps or so to the top of a boulder-strewn hilltop. The pavilion offers sea breezes and some excellent photo opportunities, as you can look towards the Macau peninsula across the Pearl River Delta's olive-brown waters. The straight white ribbon of the Macau-Taipa Bridge will lead your eyes towards the city skyline, dominated as always by the Macau Tower. On your far left you can see the new Sai Van Bridge, and on your far right the Friendship Bridge.

Climb back down to the main trail and turn left. A short walk will bring you to Taipa Monument, which consists of a staircase zigzagging downhill past a series of bas-relief sculptures that depict Macau's history. View the monument if you wish, but remember you will have to climb back up the stairs to continue your walk. Your energy is probably better spent continuing along the trail, which will offer views of the horse track, the COTAI Strip, and the Lotus Bridge that crosses over to the Chinese mainland.

As you follow the trail make sure that you stop at the exercise area, which features a special foot-massage treatment consisting of up-ended beach rocks cemented into a bed of concrete. The idea is to walk in stocking feet over the rocks, which feels somewhat like walking over a bed of very blunt nails. The experience takes stamina, but your feet really do feel better once you are done.

Once your feet have been properly rejuvenated, continue walking around Taipa Pequena Hill until you return to the Chinese pavilion. Take the trail spur down to the street, and turn right on Estrada Lou Lim Ieok. Walk a short distance until you see the gates of the Pou Tai Un Buddhist Monastery on the left-hand side of the street.

Pou Tai Un Buddhist Monastery

As the largest temple on Taipa Island, this multilevel complex offers local Buddhists the equivalent of one-stop shopping. Here they can worship in an assortment of Buddhist temples devoted to various deities, saints, and esteemed monks, with a shrine devoted to Kun Iam thrown in for good measure. To top it all off, they can enjoy a vegetarian meal with the monks, who grow their own greens and offer very reasonable prices. You are more than welcome to join the monks for lunch in their ground-floor cafeteria, as well as explore the temple's enchanting hillside tangle of carp ponds, moon gates, gardens, pavilions, and prayer halls. *(Restaurant open daily 11 a.m. to 8 p.m. Vegetarian dishes MOP$30 to 40.)*

From the monastery, return to Estrada Lou Lim Ieok and retrace your steps to the traffic circle by the New Century Hotel. From there you can easily catch a bus or taxi to Coloane Island *(see chapter seven)* or back across the bridge to downtown Macau. You can also walk down Avenida Dr. Sun Yat-Sen to Taipa Village. If you wish to visit the Taipa Fort and Memorial Garden *(see pg. 112)*, you can either flag a taxi or walk from the monastery by heading east on Estrada Lou Lim Ieok.

TAIPA TEMPLE WALK

TAIPA FORT AND THE MEMORIAL GARDEN

This old colonial fort does not really fit into any walking itinerary, and neither does the adjacent monument to Portuguese sailors blown up in 1850—but history buffs will find both landmarks worth a visit nonetheless.

Since its construction in 1847 Taipa Fort has gone through many incarnations. The Portuguese originally built the fort to cement their claim to the three islands that now comprise modern-day Taipa. The local islanders hardly minded this land grab, as their fishing vessels had been suffering from pirate attacks. They funded the construction of the fort in the hopes the Portuguese garrison would bring the pirates to heel. Eventually Portuguese ships did in fact reduce the threat of piracy, and by 1900 the fort no longer had much military use. The colonial administration remodeled the fort as a summer residence for the governor of Macau. In later years the fort also served as the Taipa police station. At that time the sea still lapped against the front walls of the fort, but land

reclamation for the Pier Garden, a formal European-style affair complete with topiary shrubs, later extended the shoreline out from the battlements. The approach road to the Sai Van Bridge has now pushed the shoreline even further away from the fort, which today houses the Scout Association of Macau. Many of the fort's military features still remain, however, including the gate, sentry boxes, the gunpowder magazine, and a cannon forged by a Boston company in 1855.

The adjacent Memorial Garden—not to be confused with the Pier Garden—commemorates the explosion of the Portuguese naval frigate *D. Maria II*, the most spectacular of Macau's many accidental detonations. On October 29, 1850, an explosion in the warship's gunpowder magazine blew the vessel to pieces, killing 188 crewmen, three hapless French prisoners in the ship's brig, and 40 unlucky Chinese on nearby sampans. Though 36 crewmen ashore escaped death, only one crewman aboard the ship survived—a cabin boy named Jose Francisco Barbosa. The sinking of the *D. Maria II* remains one of Macau's greatest tragedies, though hardly the city's only accidental blast. Taipa's cemeteries, in fact, are full of people killed in fireworks factory explosions.

Our Lady of Carmel Church stands atop a hill in Taipa Village.

The Pier Garden and Memorial Garden remain open to the public, but Taipa Fort is not, though the Scout Association might not object if you want to have a quick look at the battlements. A taxi is your best option for getting to the fort and gardens, which can be found on the northeastern side of Taipa. *(See map on pg. 109.)* If you have the time and the ambition, the fort is a walkable distance from Taipa Village or the traffic roundabout that begins the Taipa Temple Walk.

Learning the Local Lingo

Cantonese is fiendishly difficult for native English speakers to learn because it is a tonal language, meaning that words must be spoken in certain tones; get the tones wrong and you are speaking gibberish. So even if you can master the pronunciation of a word, which is no easy task in itself, you still have to master the tone of that word as well. If you just want to try out a few phrases of Cantonese, my advice is to forget the tones and focus on getting reasonably close to the correct pronunciation. When you speak the simplified atonal phrases below, Cantonese speakers will probably understand you based on the context of your words, even though you are not speaking in the proper tones. The best way to master the tonal pronunciation of these phrases is to ask a Cantonese speaker to repeat each phrase a few times.

Hello, how are you?: *Nei hou ma?*

Fine: *Gei ho.*

Thank you: *M goy.* (When thanking someone for what they have done for you. Say *do jeh* when thanking for a gift.)

Good morning: *Jou san.* (This one is perhaps the easiest phrase to learn.)

Goodbye: *Bye-bye.* (This English phrase has been incorporated into Cantonese.)

Cheers: *Yum sing!*

Oh no! Eek!: *Ai ya!* (Very common Cantonese phrase.)

Dragons stand guard over graves at the United Chinese Cemetery on Taipa Island.

Devotional figurines fill a shrine at the Pou Tai Un Buddhist monastery on Taipa Island.

TAIPA ISLAND: MACAU'S SUBURB

Coloane Island: Macau's Countryside

A day trip to Coloane features black-sand beaches, Chinese junk builders,
hilltop hiking trails, and sleepy village squares.

Unexpected juxtapositions jam the streets of Macau with an almost hallucinatory intensity. After all, this is a city where you can hear the bells of a Catholic church while simultaneously smelling the joss smoke of a Taoist temple—and you can do this while standing on a street full of Portuguese and Chinese shop signs, no less. In a city full of fascinating contrasts, however, the difference between the urban Macau peninsula and the green island of Coloane stands out as particularly striking. The built-up and paved-over Macau peninsula boasts one of the world's highest population densities, but just three miles away the quiet island of Coloane can barely muster 5,000 residents.

Coloane's sparse population and lush greenery stem from the island's traditional isolation as well as its relatively recent incorporation into Macau. After all, the Portuguese did not claim Coloane until 1864, some 300 years after the founding of the colony. The Portuguese saw little of value on Coloane itself, but by unilaterally taking over the island they gained control of the vital deep-water anchorage between Coloane and Taipa.

With the anchorage secured, the Portuguese maintained only the most halfhearted of grips on Coloane. For the local Chinese, island life more or less carried on as before. They kept to themselves and earned a living primarily from the sea through salt production, junk building, and fishing. Island specialties included oyster sauce and shrimp paste as well as salted fish, which can still be found on sale today in Coloane Village. Piracy remained another specialty, and though relatively few locals took up the buccaneer's sword, those that did wreaked considerable havoc.

The pirates who used Coloane as a base of operations continued to cause trouble until as late as 1910, when they kidnapped a number of children from Macau and Canton (Guangzhou) and demanded sizeable ransoms from their families. After receiving tips on the location of the pirates, the Portuguese military launched a rescue operation spearheaded by the gunboats *Patria*

Lead photo description on page 191

and *Macau*. After several days of shooting, Portuguese soldiers succeeded in freeing the children and ridding the island once and for all of pirate gangs.

Despite the end of the pirate scourge, Coloane remained relatively remote from the heart of colonial Macau. Traditionally, in fact, the island could only be reached by boat. In 1968, however, the new causeway linking Taipa and Coloane made it possible to drive between the two islands. However, direct road access from Coloane to peninsular Macau had to wait until 1974, with the opening of the Macau-Taipa Bridge.

But while the Macau-Taipa Bridge triggered large-scale development on Taipa, Coloane remained a sleepy backwater with a rural character. Residents of Coloane Village, the island's only community of any size, showed little inclination to change from their traditional way of life. No casinos went up on the island, much of which the colonial administration wisely designated as protected natural park. A determined government reforestation program planted over a half-million trees in this parkland between 1982 and 1996 alone, reversing centuries of deforestation. Today the island has more acres of forest than at any time in recent history. This re-greening of Coloane counts as one of the very few positive environmental stories in Macau, a city where development usually trumps conservation.

Today Coloane still serves as Macau's green zone. Less than one percent of Macau's population lives on the island, which has just one village, a few luxury villas, and a modest sprinkling of medium-rise apartment blocks. Coloane's size makes its green environment all the more significant, as the island ranks as the largest of Macau's three districts. According to the Macau Cartography and Cadastre Bureau, Coloane had a landmass of about three square miles (7.6 sq. km) in 2004, but subsequent land-reclamation projects have further increased the size of the island.

In a process many view as inevitable, these land-reclamation schemes continue to threaten Coloane's rural character. The A-Ma Cultural Village now mars the slopes of the island's largest park. The Ka Ho container port and the four-stack electrical power station operate on the northeast side of the island, completely destroying its once scenic beach-lined coast. The northeast coast has been lost to reclaimed land zoned for industrial use, while luxury villas continue to pop up along the southern coast more quickly than shoots of bamboo.

All of these projects are dwarfed by the giant COTAI Strip development project, however. Built by American-owned Las Vegas Sands on a two square mile (4.7 sq. km) swath of reclaimed land between Taipa and Coloane, the COTAI Strip project will center on the US$1.8 billion Venetian hotel and casino. The entire project will be big enough to qualify as a small city, effectively dwarfing Coloane and ending its traditional isolation from the rest of Macau.

Despite such large-scale development projects, however, Coloane has managed to hold on to a quieter and greener way of life that contrasts dramatically with the rest of Macau. Coloane has evolved into the city's casino-free playground—a place to go to the beach, hike green trails, have barbeques, and pursue other outdoor activities impossible on either Taipa or peninsular Macau. The peaceful lanes of Coloane Village, meanwhile, take urban residents back in time to a simpler age free of modern-day pressures, an age endowed with the Cantonese equivalent of what Americans call traditional family values. An older way of life truly survives in Coloane Village, a living museum where the modern world has been unobtrusively integrated into a labyrinth of streets too narrow for cars. It is for these reasons—the nostalgic charm of Coloane Village as well as the island's green parkland and black-sand beaches—that I highly recommend a visit to Coloane.

COLOANE VILLAGE WALK

A visit to sleepy Coloane Village, with its Portuguese town square and Chinese back alleys lined with timeworn shops and houses, can be a truly magical experience.

Taxis are the most convenient way to get to Coloane Village, and with MOP$60 fares from downtown Macau, reasonably priced. Buses provide frequent service to Coloane Village, but they move much more slowly than taxis. In addition, Coloane's narrow roads necessitate the use of minibuses rather than the full-sized equivalent, so the machines frequently run with full seats—leaving you standing in the aisle and trying to keep your balance each time your bus whizzes around a traffic circle like a ball on a roulette wheel. Still, you can't beat the price. Buses 21, 21A, 25, and 26A go from downtown Macau to Taipa and on to Coloane Village (MOP$4) or Hac Sa Beach (MOP$5). Bus 15 runs only between Taipa and Coloane (MOP$2.8). All buses will conveniently drop you at **President Antonio Ramalho Eanes Square** in Coloane Village.

The garden-filled square honors a military officer stationed in Macau who went on to become Portugal's president after the 1975 coup that restored democracy to that country. Rather than a bust of the president, however, the square features a somewhat incongruous statue of cupid, complete with splashing fountain.

From the bus stop, walk on over to **Lord Stow's Bakery** on the northwest corner of the square. After stopping in for some of the bakery's renowned egg tarts, continue on towards the waterfront. When you reach the seaside Avenida de Cinco de Outubro, turn left on this tree-lined boulevard and walk until you see Largo Eduardo Marques, better known as Church Square and the center point of Coloane Village.

The Coloane Village Walk begins at Church Square. However, given the compact nature of the village, you could disregard my suggested walking route and simply start wandering through the maze of lanes and alleyways that collectively comprise what may well be the most traditional neighborhood in all of Macau. In the process you will likely stumble upon the various temples and other landmarks included in the walking route anyhow.

You will find that the village has a haphazard feel to it that often borders on shabby, with dilapidated

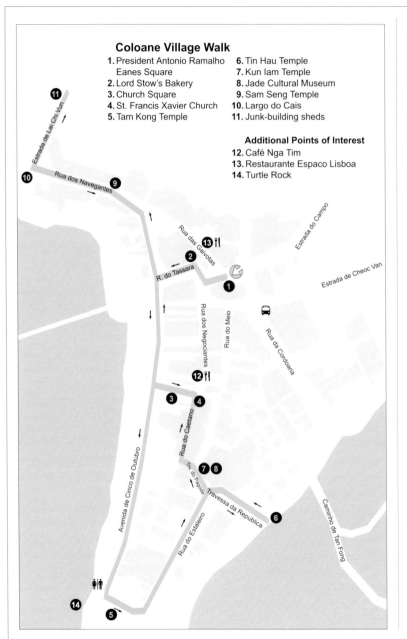

Coloane Village Walk

1. President Antonio Ramalho Eanes Square
2. Lord Stow's Bakery
3. Church Square
4. St. Francis Xavier Church
5. Tam Kong Temple
6. Tin Hau Temple
7. Kun Iam Temple
8. Jade Cultural Museum
9. Sam Seng Temple
10. Largo do Cais
11. Junk-building sheds

Additional Points of Interest

12. Café Nga Tim
13. Restaurante Espaco Lisboa
14. Turtle Rock

COLOANE VILLAGE WALK

COLOANE VILLAGE WALK

old houses awaiting restoration leaning against battered shophouses begging for a paint job. All this just adds to the special atmosphere of a village that has evolved with the times—switching from fishing to tourism, for example—while still remaining true to itself.

As you explore, keep an eye out for the little altars scattered alongside the lanes of the village. These brightly painted niches house small statues of various deities, especially Tou Tei, the earth god. Local residents place smoking joss sticks and other offerings on these altars in the hope of receiving protection, prosperity, good luck, and good health.

Watch for *feng shui* mirrors mounted above the doors of local homes as well. These mirrors range from unadorned little rectangles to ornately framed circles, but all serve the same protective function. Basically, any evil spirit seeking to enter a house will be frightened away by its own reflection in the *feng shui* mirror hanging atop the door frame.

Church Square
(Largo Eduardo Marques)

Start your walk at Church Square. Perhaps the most pleasant of the European-style plazas in Macau, this diminutive square often has a somnolent, lost-in-time feel to it. A wavy pattern of tiles reminiscent of Senate Square paves the plaza, but

this Portuguese *largo* lacks the bustle of its larger counterpart in downtown Macau. During a hot summer afternoon, in fact, the sun-washed plaza can be utterly deserted. Somehow this only adds to the charm of this little rectangle of old Europe that has been quite literally plopped down on China's doorstep.

You can see China from Church Square, after all. If you look down the length of the plaza and across Avenida de Cinco de Outubro, you will see the Pearl River seawall and the channel separating Coloane from Guangdong Province. You can watch the boat traffic—a procession of police launches, small ferries, and tug-barge combos—and peer across the river to mainland China.

At the far end of the square stands St. Francis Xavier Church, while at the foot of the plaza a small monument commemorates the 1910 victory over the last pirate band on Coloane. The *largo* takes its name from Captain Eduardo Marques, governor of Macau at the time, though few locals care. They almost universally refer to the plaza as Church Square.

The square comes to life in the evening as diners eat alfresco at the popular Café Nga Tim, where they feast on seafood and chilled white wine. A leisurely outdoor meal on Church Square may well be one of the most enjoyable experiences you can have in Macau.

St. Francis Xavier Church

St. Francis Xavier Church stands at the far end of Church Square and remains Coloane's most well-known landmark. The modest size of the church fits in well with the small scale of the village, and its light-yellow façade nicely complements the arcades lining the square. As churches go in Macau, this one has a relatively short history, having been built in 1928. However, the church had the honor of serving as a repository for one of Catholicism's most holy relics—the arm bone of St. Francis Xavier.

The famed Jesuit Francis Xavier proselytized his way across the Portuguese colonial trading network in the sixteenth century. This devout Basque converted locals to the faith in Goa, Malacca, and Japan before turning his fervor towards China. En route to China, however, Xavier died on an island near Macau in 1552. A bone from his right arm—considered a holy relic—was sent from Goa to Macau somewhere between 1618 and 1634. Originally kept in St. Paul's, the bone survived the blaze that leveled the church in 1835. Various churches, cathedrals, and seminaries then took custody of the soot-covered bone for many years, before sending it on to St. Francis Xavier Church in a procession featuring Chinese musicians playing "When the Saints Go Marching In." Along with the sacred arm bone, the church also housed the bones of seventeenth-century Japanese and Vietnamese Catholic martyrs. Today St. Francis Xavier's well-traveled arm bone has been returned to St. Joseph's Seminary, while the bones of the other martyrs rest in the Crypt and Sacred Art Museum located beneath the ruins of St. Paul's Church.

Tam Kong Temple

At the waterfront end of Church Square, turn left on Avenida de Cinco de Outubro. Follow this seaside thoroughfare past the colonial-era *biblioteca* (public library) until you reach the bright-red Tam Kong Temple at the southern end of the village. Built in 1862 to honor the Taoist god of seafarers, the temple faces a small square once used for the island's salt-making industry. In those days the square would have sloped down to a sandy beach where fishermen landed the day's catch. Today the seawall blocks access to the water and you won't see much fishing in Coloane. You can still see plenty of boat traffic, however, as well as mainland China across the channel.

For many years the Tam Kong Temple housed a four-foot-long (1.2 m) dragon boat replica carved from a whalebone. The boat came complete with a little wooden crew in lucky red outfits, and had been presented

123

to the temple by grateful local fishermen wishing to honor Tam Kong. This unusual feature of the temple can now be seen at the Macau Museum.

Two stone lions stand guard on each side of the temple door to drive off evil spirits. These lions pull sentry duty outside most temples as well as banks, homes, and other buildings. They always come in pairs, though there is really only one way to tell the male from the female—by looking under their paws. The male lion will always have a ball under his paw that symbolizes the world, while the female will always have a baby lion under her paw.

Tin Hau Temple

From the square outside the Tam Kong Temple, head up Rua do Estaleiro. Turn right on Travessa da Republica, which will take you to the Tin Hau Temple. This temple dates to 1677, making it the oldest on the island. A relic of Coloane's largely defunct fishing industry, the temple is devoted to the protector of seafarers, Tin Hau—also known as A-Ma.

Like most temples in Macau, the Tin Hau Temple also honors a variety of other deities. Along with Tin Hau, you can find statues of Kuan Tai (a warrior god), Choi Pac Seng Kuan (god of wealth), Se Chic Tai Wong (god of society), Wa To (god of medicine), and Lou Pan (god of

carpenters). No matter what your problem, you can likely find a deity who can help you at this temple.

Kun Iam Temple

Retrace your steps back down Travessa da Republica and turn right on Rua do Estaleiro. After a very short distance, turn left down Travessa do Pagode. The Kun Iam Temple will be on your right in a little walled compound. Circular moon-gate windows in the compound walls frame the temple inside, offering one of the best photo opportunities in the village. Built in the mid-1800s, this temple is dedicated to the ever-popular Kun Iam, goddess of mercy.

Jade Cultural Museum

Next to the Kum Iam Temple you will find the small Jade Cultural Museum, a recent addition to Macau's already impressive roster of museums. If jade carvings and jewelry interest you, then stop in for a look at this classic Chinese art form. *(Open daily 10 a.m. to 5 p.m. Admission free.)*

Sam Seng Temple
(Kam Fa Temple)

From the Kun Iam Temple and Jade Cultural Museum, head back to Church Square on Rua do Caetano. At the seaside end of the square, turn right and head up Avenida de Cinco de Outubro until the street name changes to Rua dos Navegantes.

Keep walking until you see the red Sam Seng Temple on your right. Built in 1865 during the heyday of Coloane's fishing and salt industries, the temple honors a trio of powerful goddesses. Local fishermen originally dedicated the temple to Kam Fa, who could bless infants and pregnant women as well as ensure that an unborn child would be male. The Taoist goddess Wa Kong—who could frighten away evil spirits—later joined the temple, as did the Buddhist Kun Iam, goddess of mercy. As a result, the temple now caters to two different religions simultaneously—a spiritual medley typical not just of Macau but of China in general.

Largo do Cais (Dock Square)

Continue up Rua dos Navegantes to the cobbled Largo do Cais (Dock Square), where you will find a sleepy border post and a ramshackle pier. Small ferries resembling military landing craft putter across from mainland China to dock at the pier, where bored police officers give the identity documents of arriving mainland Chinese or returning Macau residents a quick once over. If your visit coincides with low tide, you can try to spot the distant outline of **Turtle Rock**, a local landmark that juts from the waters at the southern end of Coloane Village by the Tam Kong Temple.

While the square once served as the dock for the ferries that ran to Taipa and peninsular Macau, locals now know the square primarily as a place to purchase dried fish, which you can find on racks positioned around the little plaza. The circles of silver fish drying on racks make for great photos.

You can also get some decent shots of mainland China from the pier. You are not allowed out on the pier, however, as it is officially a restricted border area. The locals routinely fish off the pier, however, so if you ask the police they just might let you walk out on the pier for a quick photo or two. At dusk is best, when the smog over China renders the sinking sun a particularly brilliant orange and the distant ridgelines turn to serrated silhouettes.

Junk-building Sheds

On the far side of Largo do Cais, follow Estrada de Lai Chi Vun uphill for a short distance until you reach the island's junk-building sheds on your left. The first batch of sheds will likely be empty; continue downhill until you find the active sheds. These cavernous wooden buildings are open to the street, so you can watch local craftsmen construct brightly colored dragon boats. Rowing teams race these sleek little boats during the dragon boat festival held every June. The long, narrow boats feature a carved dragon on the bow and are propelled by a crew rowing in time to a rhythm banged on a drum mounted at the stern. Along with the dragon boats, the boat builders also assemble much larger Chinese junks made entirely of wood. These master craftsmen build rare works of art, as very few junks still sail on the Pearl River.

Do not enter the sheds unless given permission to do so, and even then use extreme caution—years of nail-studded debris litters the floor, huge beams and planks swing overhead on dubious-looking cranes, and power-saws spit fantails of sawdust like little dragons. If you think the sheds look like fire hazards, you are right. Not too long ago a number of them burned down, and signs of the blaze can still be seen in the ruined buildings on the inland side of the road.

From the junk-building sheds, retrace your route back to Church Square for a drink and/or a meal. *(For advice on where to eat, see pg. 147.)*

THE TRANS-COLOANE WALK

This route combines the three walks described below into an all-day hike across the entire island.

Ambitious hikers might consider combining all three of the walks described below into the all-day Trans-Coloane Walk. Though this sounds like a daunting proposition, Coloane's small size means that anyone in reasonably good shape can handle this extended walk with relative ease. I recommend blocking out a whole day for this hike and getting an early morning start. However, I am also assuming that you will be moving at a sightseer's pace, with lots of time for photos as well as a good long lunch. For this reason, you will want an entire day. That said, a marathon runner wishing to jog the Trans-Coloane could do so in a few hours at most.

Unless you are in excellent shape and acclimatized to excessive heat, I do not recommend trying this extended hike during the summer months. The excessive temperatures and humidity will make it hard to enjoy the experience. However, if you are a hardcore hiker, a midday midsummer

A local rides down one of Coloane Village's narrow streets.

Fish dry on a rack in Coloane Village.

THE TRANS-COLOANE WALK

trek across Coloane may be just the sort of endurance test you are looking for. *(For more on trail conditions, see "Hiking in Macau" on pg. 136.)*

COLOANE TRAIL WALK

A walk along the scenic Coloane Trail will take you to the highest point in Macau.

The Coloane Trail traces the contours of the island's western ridgeline for some five miles (8.1 km), making it the longest trail by far in Macau. Ambitious hikers can extend the length of their hike a bit by adding on the Hac Sa Reservoir Circuit and Ka Ho Height Circuit, each of which stretch for one mile (1.5 km).

Start your walk in **Seac Pai Van Park** off the *estrada* of the same name. Taxis can drop you at the park gates, where there is also a convenient bus stop. If you are riding a bus, you will see the park on your left just after going through the second traffic circle at the end of the COTAI Strip between Taipa and Coloane. You will know you have reached the park when you see a small silver plane, which sits rather incongruously in the park gardens and serves as its most prominent landmark. *(Park*

open 8 a.m. to 6 p.m. Closed Mondays. Admission free.)

Aside from the plane—flown from Lisbon in 1987 by three daring pilots—the manicured grounds also feature a Chinese herbal medicine garden, a flower garden, an orchard, a pond filled with geese and ducks, a peacock house, a small zoo, a picnic area, and the highly regarded Balichao Macanese restaurant. Be sure to bring binoculars for the aviary, as you can spot a large variety of birds, including the rare Palawan peacock and crested white pheasant. *(Open 10:30 a.m. to 4:30 p.m. Closed Mondays. Admission MOP$5.)* The park also contains the Museum of Nature and Agriculture, which focuses on Coloane's farming history as well as its natural environment. This small museum can give you some useful background information before setting out on your hike. *(Open 10 a.m. to 6 p.m. Closed Mondays. Admission free.)*

Spend time in whatever parts of the park most interest you, then pick up a trail map from the information booth at the park gates. Follow the directional signs to the start of the Coloane Trail. Once on the trail, head west towards the arboretum, with its more than 100 species of trees. After the arboretum the trail comes around a hillside and turns south, bringing Coloane Village into sight below. Soon you will reach a trail junction with signs pointing towards Cheoc

COLOANE TRAIL WALK

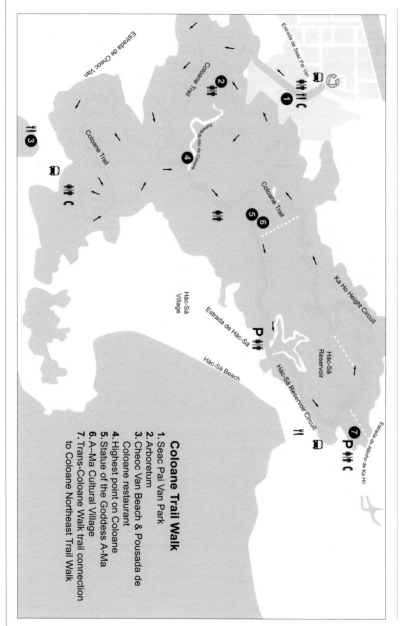

Hác-Sá
Village

Hác-Sá Beach

Coloane Trail Walk
1. Seac Pai Van Park
2. Arboretum
3. Cheoc Van Beach & Pousada de
   Coloane restaurant
4. Highest point on Coloane
5. Statue of the Goddess A-Ma
6. A-Ma Cultural Village
7. Trans-Coloane Walk trail connection
   to Coloane Northeast Trail Walk

Van (Bamboo) Beach. Bear to the right, and soon you will have great views of the beach. If the day is too hot for you, a short trail spur leads down to the beach, where you can take a quick swim before resuming your hike. The beach has changing rooms and showers as well as a large public swimming pool. For a lunch break at Cheoc Van, consider the restaurant of the Pousada de Coloane.

Eventually the Coloane Trail swings to the north, bringing the entire east-west ridgeline and the white statue of the goddess A-Ma into view. Follow the trail spur that climbs to the top of a 560-foot (170 m) wooded hill—the highest point on Coloane as well as in Macau. From this hilltop, you will see Estrada do Alto de Coloane, which you should follow to the right (east).

The winding Estrada do Alto de Coloane will lead to the dramatic hilltop **statue of the goddess A-Ma**. This graceful white sculpture complements the golden statue of Kun Iam on the waterfront of the Macau peninsula. A-Ma stands exactly 19.99 meters tall (65 feet)—a height that commemorates the year that Macau returned to China. A-Ma faces northwards so she can watch over Macau, a city she has long blessed with her protection. Though the natural beauty of the location has been somewhat spoiled by the new A-Ma Cultural Village complex, it still offers some fine views of Macau.

From the A-Ma statue, follow the trail downhill to where it connects with the Hac Sa Reservoir Circuit, which will lead you around the reservoir of the same name. Along the way you will find a recreation area by the reservoir that sells cold drinks and snacks, as well as a modern-day jungle bridge that spans the reservoir like something out of *Indiana Jones*.

As you head around the reservoir, you will reach the first junction for the Ka Ho Height Circuit on your right. If you are attempting the Trans-Coloane Walk, then you should take this junction *(see below)*. Otherwise you should continue past this junction, then take the second junction on your right and follow the Ka Ho circuit uphill until you eventually return back down to the Hac Sa Reservoir Circuit. Turn right onto the Hac Sa circuit, and the trail will soon return you to the Coloane Trail. Go right on the Coloane Trail and continue back to your starting point in Seac Pai Van Park.

Trans-Coloane Walk

If you are attempting the Trans-Coloane Walk, follow the Hac Sa Reservoir Circuit past the reservoir to the junction of the Ka Ho Height Circuit. Follow the Ka Ho circuit downhill to the Ka Ho Height Barbeque Park. From the barbeque area, turn left on Estrada do Altinho de Ka-Ho and walk until you reach the second Coloane Northeast Trail trailhead.

COLOANE NORTHEAST TRAIL WALK

A hike along the Coloane Northeast Trail takes you through some of Macau's most seldom visited parkland, though modern-day Macau will often be in distant view.

The 2.6-mile-long (4.3 km) Coloane Northeast Trail is not nearly as long or dramatic as the Coloane Trail, but this may well be its salvation, as most people seeking the great outdoors pass up this trail for the popular Coloane Trail or the island's even more popular beaches. This means you can walk the Northeast Trail in near or even complete solitude—a real trick in densely populated Macau.

Though the Coloane Northeast Trail once wound through some truly deserted green space, the trail now overlooks the COTAI Strip, the East Asian Games stadium, and the power station's smokestacks, which stand like a row of giant joss sticks.

Though surrounded by large-scale developments on three sides, the trail nonetheless offers a degree of peace and tranquility.

To reach the trail, take a taxi directly to the trailhead or get off at the bus stop just after you go through the traffic circle at the end of the COTAI Strip. From there you have to walk up Estrada do Altinho de Ka-Ho on the east side of the circle until you hit the trailhead.

After a very short walk up the trailhead, you will hit a junction; chose the left-hand option. Soon the COTAI Strip will come into view in all its construction-craned glory. From the path's higher points you will also be able to see Taipa, the international airport, and the ship-speckled waters of the Pearl River Delta.

Eventually you will come to a trail spur officially named the **Acacia Circuit**, but unofficially known as Lovers Lane. Turn onto this circuit regardless of whether you feel romantically attached to your hiking companion. This short spur leads to one of the trail's highest points— about 330 feet (100 m)—after first passing through a stretch of trail shaded by rows of—you guessed it—acacia trees. The trail loops around a small hill, offering views of the reservoir, container port, and power station. Follow Lovers Lane back down to the main trail, bearing left at the trail junction.

COLOANE NORTHEAST TRAIL WALK

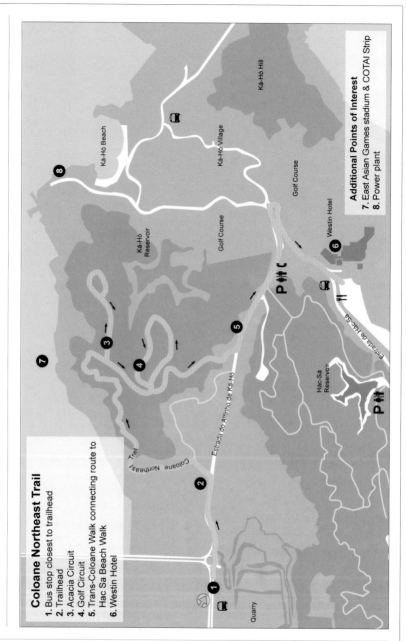

Coloane Northeast Trail

1. Bus stop closest to trailhead
2. Trailhead
3. Acacia Circuit
4. Golf Circuit
5. Trans-Coloane Walk connecting route to Hac Sa Beach Walk
6. Westin Hotel

Additional Points of Interest

7. East Asian Games stadium & COTAI Strip
8. Power plant

Ká-Hó Hill

Ká-Hó Beach

Ká-Hó Village

Golf Course

Golf Course

Ká-Hó Reservoir

Westin Hotel

Estrada do Altinho de Ká-Hó

Coloane Northeast Trail

Hác-Sá Reservoir

Estrada de Hác-Sá

Quarry

Map Legend on page 191

After a short distance another trail spur called the **Golf Circuit** will appear. Whether you count yourself a golf fan or not, take this spur, which loops around another 330-foot (100 m) summit overlooking the island's 18-hole golf course and adjacent Westin Hotel. From this height, the sand traps look like bomb craters, as if the Westin had been the victim of some poorly aimed aerial attack.

Return to the main trail and bear to the left, and a short distance later you will return to Estrada do Altinho de Ka-Ho. Turn right (west) onto the sidewalk and backtrack to the bus stop.

Trans-Coloane Walk

If you are attempting the Trans-Coloane Walk, turn left (east) on Estrada do Altinho de Ka-Ho and head downhill. When you reach a traffic circle, bear to the right and follow Estrada de Hac Sa to the Westin Hotel and Hac Sa Beach.

HAC SA BEACH WALK

Shuck your shoes and take a leisurely stroll along a black-sand beach on the South China Sea.

Stretching for three-quarters of a mile (1.2 km) in a gentle crescent, Hac Sa Beach offers Macau residents a seaside retreat from their hectic urban lives. Most locals say Hac Sa is the best of the three strips of sand on Coloane, as it is much larger than scenic Cheoc Van Beach. Ka Ho Beach, meanwhile, has been lost to the power plant and container port.

Start your walk at the **Westin Hotel**, an obvious landmark that anchors the north end of the beach. Taxis can drop you directly at the hotel, and there is a bus stop there as well. If you need a restorative beverage, stop in at the Westin's colonial-style Porto Bar with its seaside views. *(Open daily 12 to 3 p.m. and 5 p.m. to 1 a.m.)*

From the Westin, walk south along Hac Sa (Black Sand) Beach. The sable sand and silty water knock Hac Sa out of the running for Asia's most beautiful beach. Despite the black sands and olive-brown waves, however, the water is safe for swimming and locals

HAC SA BEACH WALK

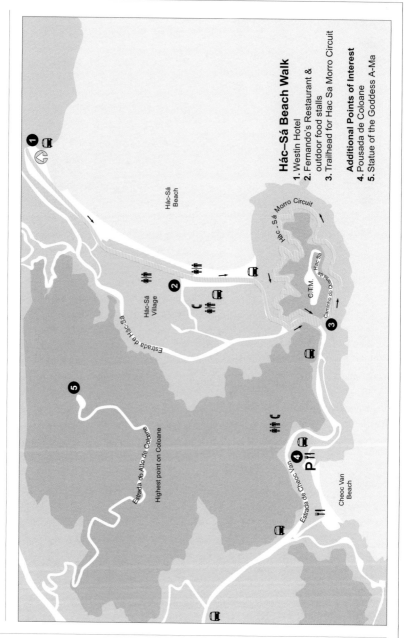

Hác-Sá Beach Walk

1. Westin Hotel
2. Fernando's Restaurant & outdoor food stalls
3. Trailhead for Hac Sa Morro Circuit

Additional Points of Interest

4. Pousada de Coloane
5. Statue of the Goddess A-Ma

Hác-Sá Beach

Hác - Sá Morro Circuit

Hác-Sá Village

Estrada de Hác-Sá

C.T.M.

Caminho do Caetano

Hác-Sá

Estrada do Alto de Coloane

Highest point on Coloane

Estrada de Cheoc Van

Cheoc Van Beach

do not hesitate to dive right in. On a very clear day—and summer haze and mainland Chinese smokestacks ensure there aren't very many of those—you can just make out the mountains of Lantau Island in Hong Kong.

As you walk along the sand you will soon reach the wooded park lining the southern half of the beach. Like all parks in Macau, this one is well maintained, with manicured topiary shrubs in the shape of elephants and modern art sculptures gleaming in the sun. Rows of trees offer much-needed shade on hot days. Find a park bench and listen to the rustle of the wind in the leaves and the rhythmic pound of the surf.

The park—which is technically two separate parks, though you would never know it—comes well equipped with swimming pools, playgrounds, tennis and badminton courts, sports fields, and a miniature golf course for those unable to afford the green fees over at the full-sized course behind the Westin. You can also rent wind surfers or jet skis. A variety of vendors operating out of kiosks and little carts sell cold drinks and inexpensive seafood snacks so popular you may have to wait in line for them on weekends. The picnic area is a nice spot to eat an alfresco takeout lunch, though several restaurants along the beach also offer outdoor dining areas. *(For advice on where to eat, see pg. 147.)*

Follow the short access road at the southern end of the beach until you reach Estrada de Hac Sa. Turn left on Estrada de Cheoc Van, and at the next intersection turn left on Caminho do Quartel de Hac Sa (Hac Sa Barracks Road). You will immediately see the trailhead for the **Hac Sa Morro Circuit**. This easy 1.3-mile (2.15 km) trail runs around a rocky, overgrown headland, offering good views of Hac Sa Beach and the South China Sea. Keep an eye out for the simian profile of Monkey Rock, the trail's most notable natural feature. After a 45-minute walk, the trail will return you to your starting point and you can walk back down to the bus stop at Hac Sa Beach.

HAC SA BEACH WALK

Hiking in Macau

Macau's modest trail system might best be described as a web of pleasant nature walks and exercise paths. None of these hikes—if they can even be called that—are particularly long or difficult, with the arguable exception of the Coloane Trail. That said, Macau's summer heat and humidity can turn even the tamest trail into a sweat-soaked torture test. But regardless of the season, here's what you need to know to trek the trails of Macau.

Fitness Level

Anyone in reasonable shape can handle Macau's trails, which are either pavement, gravel, or hard-packed dirt. Some stretches of trail can give you a real workout, however, especially the long stone staircases of the Grand Taipa Trail and Coloane Trail. Summer hiking requires you to be in good shape, as the heat and humidity will sap your energy more quickly than a Lisboa Hotel slot machine will drain your moneybelt.

What to Bring

Hiking in Macau requires only the most basic of hiking gear. Good walking shoes are a must, of course. The hiking routes were designed to offer numerous photo opportunities, so you will want to carry a camera. You might also consider packing lightweight binoculars, especially for hikes overlooking the busy Pearl River or airport runway. Taking a mobile phone along is a good idea as well, though if you don't have one you can rest assured that most hikers on the trails carry mobile phones and can dial 999 for you in an emergency.

If you hike during the hot and rainy months of the year, carry a folding umbrella, which is far cooler than a waterproof jacket or rain poncho. I also recommend wearing a hat and using sunblock. Keep in mind that in direct sun a pair of light-colored cotton pants or long skirt will be cooler than shorts. They will also provide protection against insect bites, which can sometimes be a problem during the summer months. Bare ankles and shins seem particularly attractive to biting insects, so wear socks and pack some insect repellant as a backup. Above all else, make sure that you carry at least one large bottle of water per person, as it is critically important to stay hydrated. Carry more water than you think you will need.

Trail Conditions

In general Macau's trails are well maintained and equipped with public restrooms, picnic shelters, park benches, and other facilities. While a few stretches are surfaced with asphalt or paving stones, most sections of the trail consist of hard-packed dirt or loose gravel. You should expect to encounter stone staircases, a common feature of trails in Macau, as well as the occasional narrow footbridge equipped with a cable handrail.

You will not need to worry about getting lost, as all trails are well marked with bilingual (Portuguese and Chinese) directional signs and map boards. You can get trail maps at the trailheads, though they are only available in Chinese-language versions.

Macau is a safe city with a low crime rate, despite some high-profile gang violence centered on the casinos, and all trails are safe to hike during daylight hours. That said, you should still leave your valuables back in the hotel safe, carry a mobile phone if possible, and on the more remote Coloane trails, hike with at least one other person.

Weather

Macau's hiking season runs from October to March, the city's coolest months. Average temperatures are in the 60s and 70s (15–25C), though winter cold snaps from December to February can bring lows in the 50s or even upper 40s (7–15C). Rain is infrequent from October through January, but by February the number of rain days begins to increase.

Hiking during the summer months of April to September borders on the impractical due to the high heat and heavy rain. Average daily highs are in the 80s (26–32C), though Macau

suffers through plenty of days in the 90s (32–37C). The humidity further exacerbates the heat. Suffice to say that the heat in Macau can leave you feeling like you are hiking through a steamy sauna.

Rain is common during the summer months, with June the wettest month. Heavy summer downpours can leave you drenched no matter how big your umbrella or how extensive your raingear. These rainstorms can also turn unpaved sections of trail into small mountain streams. Fortunately Macau's hills aren't high enough to produce any real risk of flash floods. However, thunderstorms can be a real hazard to hikers on exposed sections of trail running along higher elevations.

On these higher trail segments you can expect slightly cooler temperatures than you would encounter at sea level, especially when compared to urban areas. You will often get a refreshing breeze as well. In winter, the wind chill may drop the temperature enough to require an extra layer, but don't expect to find any snowcapped peaks.

In recent years smog has become a weather condition in its own right. Though a problem year round, during the winter months an orangey-brown haze of pollutants can smother Macau in smog thick enough to shut down the airport. At times it can seem like you are

HIKING IN MACAU

hiking through a surreal fog that, believe it or not, can take on a certain weird beauty all its own. You definitely lose the view, however, and the impact of all that smog on your lungs is less than salubrious. Locals say that the only truly clear days follow big holidays in China, when the factories shut down and the smog blows out to sea to reveal the sky.

When to Hike

Hit the trails during the winter months of October to March if possible. However, if you travel to Macau in the summer, you don't have to entirely rule out hiking. The shorter exercise trails on Taipa are doable in the summer, though I recommend hiking in the cooler hours of early morning, as you will share the trails with the locals—a parade of dog owners, joggers, *tai chi* practitioners, and men "walking" their song birds in ornate bamboo cages. Late afternoon to sundown can be good as well, as you will meet those out for an after-work stroll. Early morning and late afternoon offer the best light for photos as well; midday shots will likely be overexposed in the overcast sunlight typical for Macau.

Regardless of the season, keep in mind that on weekends and/or holidays Coloane can be quite busy, as the city comes out to the island to play in the great outdoors. Consequently, I recommend hiking during the quieter weekdays.

COLOANE ISLAND: MACAU'S COUNTRYSIDE

St. Francis Xavier Church stands at the end of Church Square in Coloane Village.

MACANESE CUISINE: THE ULTIMATE FUSION FOOD

*To get a real taste of Macau, you have to sample its cuisine,
which mixes Portuguese, Cantonese, Indian, and African culinary influences
into a spicy Macanese blend.*

Macanese cooking might well qualify as the world's first global fusion food. After all, though based on traditional Portuguese recipes, Macanese cuisine also incorporates Cantonese, Malay, Indian, Brazilian, and African culinary traditions as well. The Macanese, goes the old saying, eat steak with chopsticks and rice with fork and spoon.

This fusion of Portuguese and assorted non-European culinary traditions stemmed largely from the Portuguese enthusiasm for miscegenation. Since so few Portuguese women made their way to Macau, the city's soldiers, sailors, and merchants found wives in their various ports of call—southern China, Japan, Vietnam, India, Timor, and elsewhere. Predictably, this produced a lot of Eurasian children, who grew up in Macau and became known as the Macanese. Less predictably, it also produced a new style of cooking that went by the same name.

This Macanese cuisine began as a makeshift attempt by Asian wives to replicate traditional Portuguese dishes for their husbands. Inevitably, however, these women incorporated their own culinary tastes and techniques into the process. This fact, combined with the use of local ingredients like turmeric, tamarind, coconut milk, and chilies, inevitably produced a hybrid cuisine that had obvious Portuguese roots, but would nonetheless never be found on a supper table in Lisbon.

This new hybrid style of cooking in Macau broke the established culinary pattern in Asian countries colonized by Western powers. In most cases, the locals ate their indigenous cuisine while the colonials ate from menus that remained exclusively French, Dutch, British, or, in the case of the Philippines, American. Indigenous and colonial food rarely wound up on the same table. Only in Macau, where the Portuguese went local with abandon, did Asian cuisine blend with European gastronomy to produce something truly new. In every other colony, indigenous and Western cuisines remained

Lead photo description on page 191

two distinctly different traditions, which is why, for example, British-ruled Hong Kong failed to produce its own Canto-English hybrid cuisine. This may also be why Hong Kong residents have traditionally taken the ferry to Macau in search of a memorable meal.

Though a multicultural mélange, Macanese cooking ultimately stems from traditional Portuguese cuisine. Macanese dishes like *pasteis de bacalhau* (codfish croquettes) and *caldo verde* (potato, kale, and sausage soup) are quintessentially Portuguese. Macanese meals invariably feature wine, which can also be ascribed to the Luso influence, as can the long siesta that follows a big lunch washed down with a carafe of *vinho verde*.

Other influences on Macanese food came from as far away as Brazil, the largest colony in the Portuguese empire. The Macanese *feijoadas*—a hearty stew of beans, pork, potatoes, cabbage, sausage, and whatever else might be on hand in the kitchen—came from Brazil, as did peanuts, green beans, sweet potatoes, and pineapples. The chilies that spice so many Macanese dishes also came from the New World.

Sailors, and the wives they picked up along the way, brought recipes from the Portuguese colonies of Angola and Mozambique in Africa as well as Goa on the Indian coast and Malacca on the present-day Malaysian peninsula. These recipes included classic Macanese dishes like *galinha Africana* (chicken cooked in chili-spiced coconut milk) and prawns cooked in a garlic and chili sauce.

The Cantonese flavored Macanese food with a host of ingredients, including ginger, cumin, shrimp paste, and soy sauce. The many varieties of Cantonese sausage replaced the often unavailable Portuguese sausages like *linguica* or *chourice* that were so beloved back in Lisbon.

Traditionally, Macanese cooking relied on family recipes handed down from mother to daughter like valuable family heirlooms. Macanese women often considered their recipes to be family secrets, so true Macanese cooking remained something you could only taste at a family meal. Macau always had Macanese restaurants, of course, but they remained a peripheral offshoot of what was essentially a highly complex form of home cooking. Many recipes did not lend themselves to restaurants, in fact, as they were slow-cooking dishes that produced large servings intended to feed entire families rather than individual diners.

Hong Kong's post-World War II emergence as an economic dynamo and the closely linked casino gambling boom in Macau changed Macanese cuisine from a food primarily eaten in Macanese homes to a restaurant food primarily consumed by foreigners from Hong Kong and elsewhere. While quite a few of the gamblers from Hong Kong came strictly for the gaming tables and had no interest in eating, much less eating well, a significant number wanted to dine in style. Macanese restaurants proliferated as a result, and soon Macanese cuisine became so well known in Hong Kong that hungry punters took the ferry over from the British colony not just to gamble, but to drink Portuguese wine and sample the local cuisine as well.

Despite Macau's handover to China in 1999 and the resulting exodus of Portuguese and Macanese from the city, the future of Macanese cuisine seems secure. While the traditional customer base has been much reduced, most of the restaurants open before the handover have managed to survive by serving local Cantonese and foreign tourists with a taste for Macanese dishes. Of course, any Macanese will tell you that the best plates are still found at family meals, with their communal dishes based on secret recipes guarded as carefully as ATM pin numbers. Whether at home or in a restaurant, however, it appears that Macau's unique cuisine will continue to simmer like a tasty stew on the stove of history.

MACANESE CUISINE: THE ULTIMATE FUSION FOOD

A vendor proudly displays his selection of dried fish, one of Macau's most well-known delicacies.

A gourmet Portuguese meal awaits at the Restaurante Espaco Lisboa in Coloane Village.

Classic Dishes of Macau

Be sure to sit down for at least one meal at a Macanese and/or Portuguese restaurant. Your repast should be a long and unhurried affair with lots of wine, preferably eaten alfresco on a patio with a view of the Pearl River and a cooling sea breeze. While you will have a wide variety of options to choose from, any meal in Macau should include some, and preferably all, of the following elements:

Vinho Verde
A chilled, slightly effervescent white wine that should accompany any and all Macanese meals.

Pasteis de Bacalhau
Generally served as an appetizer, these small codfish croquettes are a traditional favorite.

Sardinhas Fritas or Sardinhas Grelhadas
It's amazing how simply frying or grilling a bunch of sardines can result in such a tasty appetizer, especially with some olives on the side. A traditional Portuguese favorite.

Caldo Verde
Though no two versions of this "green soup" are ever quite the same, the basic ingredients are fairly consistent—potato, kale, and a Portuguese sausage like *linguica* or *chourice*.

Bacalhau
You can have your codfish served in any number of ways, but regardless of what you decide, make sure your meal includes this beloved Portuguese staple.

Gambas Grelhadas com Molho
Grilled king prawns with a sauce heavy on the garlic and chilies. If you love seafood, don't miss this one.

Galinha Africana
Known in English as spicy Macau chicken or African chicken, this dish consists of chicken baked in coconut milk, with plenty of garlic and chilies thrown in. A true Macanese dish indeed.

Feijoadas
A hearty stew of beans, pork, sausage, potatoes, cabbage, and whatever else the cook has on hand. Based on a recipe from Brazil, once Portugal's largest colony.

Pasteis de Nata (egg tart)
Probably the most well-known Macanese food, this little pie consists of an egg custard in a pastry shell. Sprinkle a dash of cinnamon on top as a traditional topping.

Bebinca de Leite
The ever-popular Macanese milk pudding.

Macanese Restaurants

To truly taste Macau, you will have to get yourself invited to a family meal in a Macanese home. If you can't swing a dinner invitation, then you can still do pretty well at one of the city's many fine Macanese and Portuguese restaurants—in many restaurants, the distinction between the two cuisines is somewhat blurry. Here are some recommendations for good eating:

Macau Peninsula

Os Gatos

Perhaps the most atmospheric alfresco restaurant in Macau, as its tree-shaded patio sits atop the battlements of a seventeenth-century fort. Pousada de Sao Tiago, Avenida da Republica. 378-111. Open 11:30 a.m. to 11:30 p.m. *(See map on pg. 63.)*

Institute for Tourism Studies Educational Restaurant

Very affordable Portuguese and Macanese dishes prepared by apprentice chefs. Pousada de Mong-Ha, Rua de Francisco Xavier Pereira. 561-252. Open 12:30 p.m. to 3:00 p.m. and 7:00 p.m. to 10:30 p.m. Closed weekends. *(See map on pg. 160.)*

Restaurante A Lorcha

289A Rua do Almirante Sergio. 313-195. Open 12:30 p.m. to 3:00 p.m. and 6:30 p.m. to 11:00 p.m. Closed Tuesdays. *(See map on pg. 67.)*

O Porto Interior

Portuguese and Macanese. 259B Rua do Almirante Sergio. 967-770. Open noon to 11:30 p.m. *(See map on pg. 67.)*

Restaurante Litoral

Eat here for true Macanese fare. 261A Rua do Almirante Sergio. 967-878. Open noon to 3:00 p.m. and 6:00 p.m. to 10:30 p.m. *(See map on pg. 67.)*

Praia Grande

Serves gourmet Portuguese cuisine inside and drinks outside from a kiosk stationed in a pleasant plaza opposite the restaurant. 10A Praca de Lobo D'Avila, Avenida da Praia Grande. 973-022. Open noon to 11 p.m. *(See pg. 63.)*

Clube Militar de Macau

Built in 1870 and restored in 1994, this elegant building served as a club for Portuguese military officers before becoming a restaurant. 975 Avenida da Praia Grande, beside the Jardim de Sao Francisco. 714-000. Open 7:00 p.m. to 11:00 p.m. *(See map on pg. 72.)*

Riquexo

Despite the informal, cafeteria-style setup, this restaurant serves up some of the most authentic Macanese food in the city. Dishes change daily. 69 Avenida de Sidonio Pais. 565-655. *(See map on pg. 53.)*

Ali Curry House

Popular with the lunch-hour crowd, this inexpensive restaurant serves a mix of Macanese, Portuguese, Cantonese, and assorted other dishes. 4 Avenida da Republica. 555-865. Open 12:30 p.m. to 11:30 p.m. *(see map on pg. 63.)*

Taipa

Estalagem

Portuguese fine dining. 410 Estrada Governador Albano de Oliveira. 821-041. Open noon to 3 p.m. and 6 p.m. to whenever the last diners finish dessert. *(See map on pg. 109.)*

O Infante

Small, traditional Portuguese restaurant with friendly service. Located in the atmospheric lanes of Taipa Village. Rua das Virtudes. 827-421. *(See map on pg. 101.)*

Pou Tai Un Buddhist Monastery

No-frills vegetarian restaurant on ground floor of the monastery. 2 Estrada Lou Lim Ieok. 811-038. Open 11 a.m. to 8 p.m. *(See map on pg. 109.)*

Coloane

Restaurante Espaco Lisboa

Located down a quiet lane in Coloane Village, this restaurant is one of my favorite places for a leisurely multi-course lunch. Named in honor of the Portuguese capital and located in a renovated two-story shophouse. Chef Antonio Neves Coelho will even open your

champagne bottle with a sword. 8 Rua das Gaivotas, Coloane Village. 882-226. Open noon to 3:00 p.m. and 6:30 p.m. to 10:00 p.m. weekdays; noon to 10:30 p.m. weekends. *(See map on pg. 121.)*

Pousada de Coloane

Friendly family-run Portuguese restaurant with verandah overlooking Cheoc Van Beach. Rua de Antonio Francisco, Coloane. 882-143. *(See map on pg. 129.)*

Café Nga Tim

Located in the center of Coloane Village on Church Square, this laidback restaurant defies easy categorization. Part sidewalk café and part seafood restaurant, with a mix of Chinese, Macanese, and Portuguese dishes. 8 Rua do Caetano, Coloane Village. 882-086. Open noon to 1 a.m. *(See map on pg. 121.)*

Fernando's

A Coloane institution serving hearty Portuguese food. 9 Praia de Hac Sa, Hac Sa Beach. 882-264. Open noon to 9:30 p.m. *(See map on pg. 134.)*

Drinking in Macau

If you have any doubts about the lasting impact of the Portuguese on Macau, go to any shop or supermarket and check out the alcohol aisle. There you will find an impressive assortment of Portuguese wines and ports, which fly off the shelves at a steady rate. Those bottles aren't going home in the duty free bags of tourists either; they are going home in the shopping bags of local residents, who have come to love a good glass of *vinho* as much as the Portuguese.

Macau has long been the little-known wine capital of Asia and the place to go for the best-priced selection of wines from Portugal and other countries. This is changing, as wine becomes more popular in Asia and the world economy makes wine more available in the continent's major cities. Still, no other city in Asia has such a deep-rooted appreciation for the red and the white. Any Macanese restaurant will have a substantial wine list, underpinned by house wines ordered by the carafe, and any supermarket will have a veritable wine cellar's worth of bottles. Basically, if you like wine, you will like Macau.

Along with their fondness for European wines, the Cantonese of Macau like their rice wine and brandy as well. You can get plenty of both in Macau in qualities that range from near rotgut to top vintage. Beer is popular, too, and while Macau won't impress true beer connoisseurs—no Asian city will—you can still drink some decent suds. Beer lovers can choose from a variety of pilsner-type beers, especially Carlsberg, San Miguel, Tsingtao, and Heineken. Keep an eye out for Macau Beer, which is the city's only true local brew, as well as imported Portuguese beers like Sagres that you probably won't find anywhere else in Asia.

As they always have, the Cantonese favor tea, particularly green and jasmine. You can try all manner of exotic herbal brews with reputed medicinal properties at specialty tea stores. Macanese coffee tends to be European in style, meaning high in quality but small in quantity. Expect a deep, rich flavor, but dinky cups that seem lilliputian compared to North American mugs. Several Portuguese-style cafés can be found on little Travessa de Sao Domingos off of Senate Square. However, Starbucks recently opened a café on the square itself, an event that promises to change the future of java in Macau.

❖   ❖   ❖

Hot tea is poured for early risers at the Long Wa Teahouse

On his way to lunch at a restaurant in Coloane Village, the author stops to pet an appreciative local cat.

Macanese Cuisine: the Ultimate Fusion Food

SHOPPING IN MACAU

*From bargain-priced street markets to upscale hotel arcades,
you will find endless browsing opportunities in Macau.*

Macau has never been known as a shopper's paradise—that honor goes to Hong Kong, its wealthy cousin across the Pearl River Delta. After all, if Hong Kong and Macau were stores, Hong Kong would be an all-purpose megamart open 24/7. Macau, on the other hand, would be a family-run specialty shop that closed at noon for a leisurely lunch followed by a long siesta.

You can still shop till you drop in Macau if you want to, though that's not really the local style. Macau is for browsers rather than power shoppers, a place where the unhurried consumer pace means you can spend an hour in a market just soaking up the ambience and then move on without buying anything, leaving neither you nor the merchants disappointed.

In Macau, you will find, shopping is not a means to an end; it is simply the end itself. In other words, you shop in Macau to enjoy the experience, not to acquire newly purchased items. You inevitably make some purchases, but these buys are just a part of the overall experience of wandering Macau's mazelike warren of narrow city streets. You go to the market to enjoy the experience rather than for the express purpose of buying what's on sale there. For this reason, this chapter focuses more on where to shop rather than what to buy once you get there.

A shop sells herbal medicines and other traditional
Chinese remedies on Rua dos Mercadores.

Lead photo description on page 191

CITY CENTER MARKET WALK

This stroll through some of Macau's oldest neighborhoods will take you to street stalls and shophouses selling everything from bootleg Nike visors to Chairman Mao alarm clocks.

Some of Macau's most vibrant shopping districts can be found around Senate Square, which despite its name resembles a triangle rather than anything close to a box or rectangle. The streets, lanes, and alleys running from the square are just as erratic, with zigzags and doglegs, uneven staircases, and unexpected name changes. All of these streets have commercial functions, which have continually evolved over the centuries into their current permutations. This walk will take you through this tangle of streets, and though you will cover relatively little ground as the crow flies, you will stroll through a number of the most intriguing market streets in the old city center. There is no better place to begin your walk than on Avenida de Almeida Ribeiro, the busy commercial thoroughfare running across the bottom of Senate Square.

Avenida de Almeida Ribeiro

Start at the **General Post Office** with its signature clock tower on the corner of Senate Square. Duck inside and you will find a specialty shop devoted to philatelists, though you don't have to be a stamp collector to appreciate the beauty of these commemorative stamp sheets depicting everything from rickshaws to roulette wheels. The prices are based on the face value of the stamps, making these stamp sheets a very good buy indeed.

After leaving the post office, walk away from Senate Square to where Avenida de Almeida Ribeiro meets Avenida da Praia Grande. On the corner you will see the Portuguese-owned **Banco Nacional Ultramarino** (National Overseas Bank). In yet another example of how well Macau can preserve a colonial structure's architecture while simultaneously modernizing it, the building's original façade now wraps around the lower floors of the highrise containing the bank's offices. Across the street you will see an architecturally unremarkable branch of the rival Bank of China. Together these two banks issue the local currency, each utilizing their own designs for the pataca notes they mint on behalf of the government of Macau. *(See "Pataca and Hong Kong Dollars: The Two Currencies of Macau" on pg. 166.)*

City Center Market Walk

1. Senate Square & General Post Office
2. Banco Nacional Ultramarino
3. Pavilions Supermercado
4. Central Plaza Mall & Wing Tai Chinese Antiquities
5. Gold dealers
6. Tak Seng On Pawnshop Museum
7. St. Dominic's Municipal Market & clothing stalls
8. Sam Kai Vui Kun Temple
9. Hong Kung Temple
10. Start of Tercena Street market
11. Camoes Garden
12. St. Anthony's Church
13. Chinese antiques shops
14. Ruins of St. Paul's Church
15. Souvenir shops
16. Chinese furniture shops

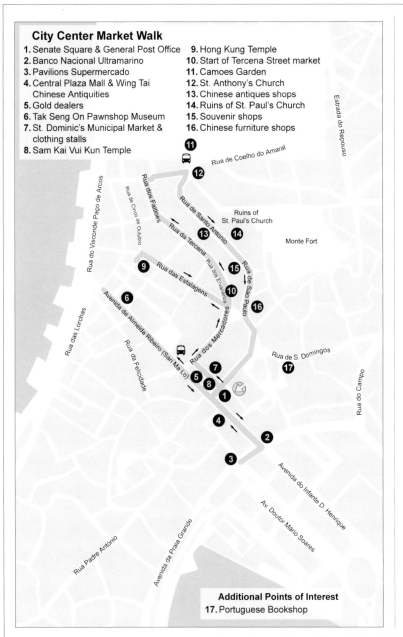

Additional Points of Interest
17. Portuguese Bookshop

Turn right on Avenida da Praia Grande and walk a short distance to the **Pavilions Supermercado** (421 Avenida da Praia Grande). In the basement you will discover a wide selection of Portuguese wines and ports, making this supermarket a good place to stock up on some inexpensive *vinho verde*. You can also browse the grocery aisles, with their shelves of imported foods from Portugal and just about everywhere else in the world. In the process, you will get a good sense of what the locals buy when they go to the supermercado. *(Open 10:00 a.m. to 9 p.m. Monday to Saturday. Sunday 11 a.m. to 8 p.m.)*

Retrace your steps up Avenida de Almeida Ribeiro on the left side of the street. You will pass the **Central Plaza Mall**, a modern emporium of designer labels that contrasts with the adjacent **Wing Tai**, a cluttered shop jammed full of dusty Chinese antiquities. Browsing the crowded aisles of Wing Tai feels like being in a museum where everything is for sale.

Continue past Senate Square. From this point on much of Almeida Ribeiro runs beneath the arcades of vintage buildings, making your window shopping atmospheric as well as sun-shaded and rain-free. These arcades featured in the 1930s Shanghai scenes of *Indiana Jones and the Temple of Doom*. As you walk in the footsteps of Harrison Ford, you will pass hotels and pharmacies as well as shops

specializing in that trio of well-known local delicacies—Macanese cookies, dried salted fish, and pressed squares of pork and beef. You will also pass shops so stuffed full of gold they look like air-conditioned treasure caves.

Macau first became known for its **gold dealers** during the Second World War, when those fleeing the Japanese occupation of Hong Kong and southern China took refuge in the neutral haven. Many of these refugees survived by selling the gold they had brought with them. Today's dealers can import gold duty free into Macau, which lets them undercut prices in other Asian cities. As many tourists from Hong Kong and Taiwan already know, if you are in the market for gold, Macau is the place to come. If you just want an unadorned hunk of the precious metal, shops post the day's price per tael of gold (1.2 troy ounces or 37.799g). All you have to do is know the weight of an ingot to figure the selling price. If you want something a bit more fancy, you can find gold rings, necklaces, decorative sculptures, spoons, fountain pens—you name it, it's been turned into gold on Avenida de Almeida Ribeiro.

As for the far less expensive salted fish, you will see them hanging with paper-covered heads outside specialty shops that also offer dried abalone, shrimp, scallops, shark fins, and just about anything else that can

A man window-shops in the NAPE District.

An array of Macau's famous meats on Rua da Felicidade.

be pulled from the South China Sea. Given this emphasis on seafood, it is no surprise that Avenida de Almeida Ribeiro ends at the Inner Harbor, now the anchorage for the city's still-sizeable fleet of black-hulled fishing vessels.

Tak Seng On Pawnshop Museum

When you reach the end of Avenida de Almeida Ribeiro at the Inner Harbor, turn around and head back towards Senate Square on the opposite side of the street. You will soon reach the new Tak Seng On Pawnshop Museum (396 Avenida de Almeida Ribeiro). Even if you aren't planning to pawn your digital camera, the museum is still worth a quick visit. The museum is housed in what used to be an actual pawnshop with the Chinese name Tak Seng On— which translates into English as the somewhat euphemistic Virtue and Success Pawnshop. The displays tell you all about the city's pawnshops, which have traditionally loaned cash to busted gamblers and other locals down on their luck. Check out the granite storage tower adjacent to the museum, where pawned gold jewelry and other loot was stored under maximum security. *(Open 10:30 a.m. to 7 p.m. Closed Mondays. Admission MOP$5.)*

St. Dominic's Municipal Market (Mercado de Sao Domingos)

When you reach Senate Square, take Rua Sul do Mercado de Sao Domingos, which is the first narrow street running off the left (west) side of the plaza opposite the white Santa Casa da Misericordia building. You will easily spot this street, which is lined by **clothing stalls** selling everything from bras to baby booties. Much of this clothing originates in the city's garment factories, many of which do not show much concern for international copyrights. Keep in mind that if it is Nike and dirt cheap, then it is also a bootleg. These brand name rip-offs may still be a great deal, but have no illusions about their authenticity. Expect the cheaper T-shirts to shrink into bizarre shapes suitable for only the most deformed of human physiques.

Scattered among the clothing vendors you will also find a few stalls selling jade jewelry, sculptures, and other objects. You won't have to worry about whether the jade is real or not, but you should be concerned about the relative quality of the jade. Only experts know the difference in grades, so don't buy any high-priced jade items unless you know what you are doing. That said, the cheaper jade jewelry and carved figurines make great presents for all those folks back home you owe gifts to.

In the midst of all these street stalls you will find the little **Sam Kai Vui Kun Temple** as well as the Mercado de Sao Domingos. This multilevel market building hosts the modern version of a traditional Chinese market, with each floor split into dozens of small stalls selling fresh produce, seafood and meats, canned foods, spices and seasonings, and just about anything else local families could need to prepare their daily meals. Be warned that the butcher's floor looks and smells like an abattoir, complete with skinned cow heads and various internal organs laid out on display for eager buyers.

Rua dos Mercadores

On the far side of the Mercado de Sao Domingos you will find Rua dos Mercadores. Take a right on this narrow street, which is well-known for its fruit vendors. This is the place to pick up guavas, rambutans, and mangosteens for the best prices, though the street contains businesses devoted to much more than just fruit. You will find *pastelarias* (bakeries) and *lavandarias* (laundries) as well as shops selling watches, wedding dresses, hardware, herbal medicines, jade figurines, and pet songbirds. Make your way up Mercadores and turn left on Rua das Estalagens.

Rua das Estalagens

Rua das Estalagens is a narrow street with shops devoted to electronics and small appliances, hardware, clothing, and pet birds. This is a good street for purchasing chops, the hand-carved Chinese-name stamps still in use throughout the city. You can have your own personal chop custom made for a very reasonable price.

When you reach Rua de Cinco de Outubro, turn left at the Hong Kung Temple.

Hong Kung Temple

This temple sits on the corner of Rua das Estalagens and Rua de Cinco de Outubro. Built in 1750, the temple honors Kuan Tai, god of war and wealth. The temple and its square once stood at the center of Cantonese commerce along the shores of the Inner Harbor, though land reclamation has since left this quiet neighborhood landlocked. The area is often touted as a clothing market, but these days you won't find much for sale. Enjoy the pleasant square opposite the temple instead.

From the Hong Kung Temple, retrace your steps back up Rua das Estalagens and turn left onto little Rua dos Ervanarios.

Tercena Street

Make your way up pedestrian-only Rua dos Ervanarios, one of the most traditional streets in Macau. Shopkeepers in this area used to attract attention to their wares by banging two pieces of metal together, but these days the somnolent quiet of the street makes for pleasant browsing. The somewhat marginal shops lining this street sell antiques, coins, pet fish, jade, bird cages, fighting kites, and all manner of temple-related paraphernalia, such as hell money, *feng shui* mirrors, joss sticks—you name it. A little good-natured bargaining may save you some money here, but remember that if it's cheap, it isn't antique.

Rua dos Ervanarios meets Rua da Tercena at a little triangular plaza paved in Portuguese tiles. Vendors often spread their treasures out on the plaza, with the dishware and carved jade figurines of one dealer blending into the antique colonial coins and used small appliances of the next vendor. Keep an eye out for Chairman Mao memorabilia—those ashtrays, watches, and tea cups emblazoned with the chairman's visage make for interesting souvenirs, albeit ones of questionable taste. After all, the chairman's bloody Cultural Revolution caused massive suffering and killed millions of people.

Continue down Rua da Tercena, which will switch names to become Rua dos Faitioes. When Faitioes ends at a T-junction, turn right on Calcada do Botelho and walk a short distance uphill to the square with St. Anthony's Church and Camoes Garden. Turn right down Rua de Santo Antonio.

Rua de Santo Antonio and Rua de Sao Paulo

The cobblestone Rua de Santo Antonio wraps around the hill crowned with the ruins of St. Paul's Church. Many of the shophouses lining this street have **antique stores** on the first floor that sell everything from silk dragon robes to jade dragon carvings. Browsing in these shops feels like rummaging in the attic of an old Chinese mansion. Keep in mind, however, that unless you are an expert on Chinese art and antiquities, forgeries are almost impossible to spot, so use caution when purchasing big-ticket items. You can request certificates of authenticity for antiques, though obviously the certificate can be faked even more easily than the antiquity itself.

Rua de Santo Antonio ends at the base of the staircase that leads up to the façade of St. Paul's Church. In contrast to the tasteful array of highbrow art and antiquities for sale on Rua de Santo Antonio, the **souvenir shops** clustered at the base of the stone staircase peddle an array of tacky tourist items—Guia Hill lighthouse key chains, St. Paul's T-shirts, and postcards galore. You can also find Macau street-sign magnets, which have become popular souvenirs.

Follow Rua de Sao Paulo downhill towards Senate Square. Along the way you will pass **shops selling vintage and reproduction Chinese furniture**. Here you will find lacquer screens, enclosed sedan chairs, and chests redolent of camphor. You will also find scroll paintings, bronzeware, and porcelain. The shops are well worth a browse even if you have no intention of picking up a set of ornately carved Chinese chairs. For a fee, these stores will ship your purchases home for you, even if you buy one of those heavy sedan chairs.

When you have seen enough of the furniture stores, continue down Rua de Sao Paulo to Senate Square, starting point of your walk.

RED MARKET AND THREE LAMPS DISTRICT WALK

This stroll takes you past some of Macau's more upscale shops as well as through one of its most popular street markets, with surprises along the way that range from Burmese food to Cantonese opera.

This walk takes you through a bustling commercial district where many locals do their shopping for high-end as well as cut-rate goods. Like all of Macau, the area mixes the traditional with the modern, resulting in an interesting mix of market buildings, street stalls, and upscale shops with the logos of the world's major credit cards stuck to their doors. If you want to explore a part of Macau that lies off the tourist track, and do a little shopping along the way, then this is the walk for you.

Start your walk at the Ox Warehouse on the corner of Avenida do Almirante Lacerda and Avenida do Coronel Mesquita. You can reach this trendy art gallery by bus or taxi. Alternatively, the warehouse can be reached on foot from Senate Square if you have time for an extended

RED MARKET AND THREE LAMPS DISTRICT WALK

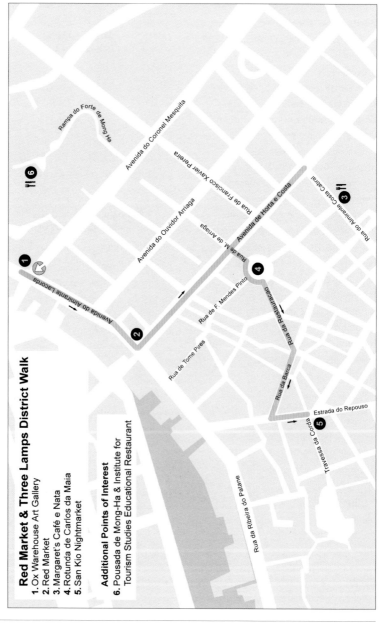

Red Market & Three Lamps District Walk
1. Ox Warehouse Art Gallery
2. Red Market
3. Margaret's Café e Nata
4. Rotunda de Carlos da Maia
5. San Kio Nightmarket

Additional Points of Interest
6. Pousada de Mong-Ha & Institute for Tourism Studies Educational Restaurant

Map labels (clockwise):
Rampa do Forte de Mong Ha
Avenida do Coronel Mesquita
Avenida do Ouvidor Arriaga
Rua de Francisco Xavier Pereira
Rua de M. de Arriaga
Avenida de Horta e Costa
Rua do Almirante Costa Cabral
Avenida do Almirante Lacerda
Rua de F. Mendes Pinto
Rua de Tome Pires
Rua da Restauração
Rua da Barca
Estrada do Repouso
Travessa da Corda
Rua da Ribeira do Patane

Map Legend on page 191

stroll. There are a number of ways to walk there—see your map for the route that best works for you.

Ox Warehouse

A former slaughterhouse converted into an art gallery, the Ox Warehouse displays the paintings, sketches, sculptures, photographs, and other work of local artists. Even if you have no intention of buying, the rotating displays of art are still worth taking in. Once you have had your fill of artwork, you can drink your fill of coffee at the café. A shop also sells CDs, books, and other items. An eclectic roster of local and international musical groups often play at the warehouse, and ticket prices are quite reasonable. *(Open noon to 7 p.m. Closed Tuesdays.)*

From the Ox Warehouse, walk two blocks south and turn right onto Avenida de Horta e Costa, where you will immediately see the Red Market.

Red Market (Mercado Vermelho)

Built in 1936, this art deco market building takes its name from its red-brick walls. Though land reclamation has left the market much further inland than it used to be, its vendors continue to sell the fresh seafood caught in the nets of Macau's fishing fleet. They also offer a broad array of fruits, vegetables, and other foodstuffs as well as cookware and kitchen utensils. Flower stands outside the market, meanwhile, sell fresh flowers brought over from China early each morning. You probably won't buy much here, but you will get to people watch as local residents pick up their fresh food for the day in this dimly lit warren of small stalls. These stalls collectively emit an unforgettable combination of smells—a pungent mix of dried fish, fresh fruit, butcher's blood, and who knows what else.

Avenida de Horta e Costa

From the Red Market, walk down Avenida de Horta e Costa. This busy thoroughfare bisects the Macau peninsula, running from the Inner Harbor to Guia Hill. On this popular shopping street you will find a mix of upscale shops specializing in clothing, shoes, electronics, jewelry, and cameras. Locals remain the target market here, as evidenced by the shops specializing in dried seafood and traditional Chinese medicine. For coffee, egg tarts, and other fresh-baked delights turn right on Rua do Almirante Costa Cabral and duck into **Margaret's Café e Nata**.

Window-shop your way down the avenue until you reach the traffic ramp for the Guia Hill Tunnel. Then cross the street and retrace your steps back to Rua de Manuel de Arriaga. Turn left and walk one block to the Rotunda de Carlos da Maia.

Three Lamps District
(Rotunda de Carlos da Maia)

This sprawling multi-block street market is hidden down a maze of narrow side streets near the Carlos da Maia traffic circle, which features the European-style wrought-iron streetlamps that gave the district its name. Some of the best shops and market stalls can be found on Rua de Manuel de Arriaga, on the north side of the circle, and Rua de Tome Pires, which is reached via Rua de Fernao Mendes Pinto on the west side of the circle. However, the whole area offers great shopping, particularly for clothing ranging in price from cut-rate to boutique. You will have the most fun if you let yourself get completely lost and wander from stall to shop without worrying about which direction you are heading.

While this popular street market has become locally famous for its authentic and inexpensive southeast Asian food, it has become particularly well known for its Burmese cuisine. Starting in the 1960s, thousands of Burmese Chinese fled the violence in their own country and settled in this neighborhood, living alongside ethnic Chinese refugees from Indonesia, Cambodia, and other conflict-plagued countries in Asia. Their influence gives the market a pan-Asian feel scented with Burmese curry, much of it cooked in informal market stalls.

San Kio Nightmarket

If it's a weekend evening and you are still going strong, you can take a short backstreet stroll over to the San Kio Nightmarket. The simplest route from the Carlos da Maia traffic circle takes you west on Rua da Restauracao until you hit Rua da Barca. Go right on Barca to Estrada do Repouso and turn left on this major thoroughfare. One block south turn right on Travessa da Corda, where you will find the San Kio Nightmarket.

Organized by a local neighborhood association, this little market takes place outside the Lin Kai Temple. The temple dates to the 1600s and honors Wah Kwong, a deity tasked with the double duty of protecting his devotees from fire and serving as the patron of Cantonese opera. Unsurprisingly, perhaps, the market stages Cantonese operas—a colorful and noisy experience not to be missed—and an old firehouse hosts the Macau Fire Service Museum just a few blocks away.

The market hardly warrants a special shopping trip, but if you are in the area anyhow, you might as well stop by and experience this cheerful neighborhood market offering a somewhat random mix of toys, clothing, antiques, and household goods. You will also find food stalls selling tasty, inexpensive, and sometimes unidentifiable snacks. *(Nightmarket open Friday and Saturday, 5:00 p.m. to 11:00 p.m.)*

STREET FAIRS, MUNICIPAL MARKETS, AND HOTEL ARCADES

Macau has many more places to browse, ranging from posh hotel arcades to humble municipal markets.

Municipal Markets

The city has at least nine municipal markets, which are public buildings filled with privately owned stalls selling fresh fruit, vegetables, meat, and fish. St. Dominic's Municipal Market *(see pg. 156)* just off of Senate Square is the market most commonly encountered by foreign tourists, while the Red Market *(see pg. 161)* remains the most architecturally interesting. However, all of the other municipal markets offer just as wide a range of foods.

Municipal market buildings are generally divided into sections devoted to a certain kind of merchandise. Each section contains dozens of small stalls, all run by a different vendor but selling similar goods—fruit in one section, meat in another, for example. These markets tend to be cramped mazes full of narrow aisles lined with piles of fruit, pyramids of canned goods, mounds of vegetables, ranks of soy sauce bottles, and racks of meat. Those with sensitive noses should stay away, as municipal markets never fail to produce some powerful smells.

Municipal markets cater to the Cantonese palate, which can make exploring them an interesting cross-cultural experience, though probably not of the shopping sort. Fresh fruit and other snacks aside, you won't find much of interest here to buy. However, you will see how neighborhood families purchase their fresh ingredients for home-cooked meals. This can range from live chickens to tropical fruit so exotic it looks like it came from another planet.

Other than St. Dominic's Market and the Red Market, the other municipal market that visitors are most likely to visit is the large St. Laurence Municipal Market (Mercado Municipal de Sao Lourenco) on Rua de Joao Lecaros. Out on the islands both Taipa Village and Coloane Village have small municipal markets, respectively located on Largo dos Bombeiros and Largo do Presidente Antonio Ramalho Eanes.

Weekend Art Fair

Located at the Nam Van Lakeside Plaza on the Avenida da Praia Grande, directly across from the pink colonial-era headquarters of the Macau SAR, this newcomer to the local market scene specializes in arts and crafts. *(See map on pg. 63.)* Many of the items on sale here are one-of-a-kind, including everything from eggshell carvings to the inevitable tie-dyed shirts. You can also get your own personal "chop"—the hand-carved Chinese-name stamps still widely used in Macau. If you visit the market at either 8:30 or 9:30 p.m., you can catch the impressive cybernetic fountain display on Nam Van Lake, which features laser lighting and jets of water shooting as high as 260 feet (80 m). *(Open 4:30 p.m. to 10:30 p.m. on weekends and public holidays.)*

Taipa Village Sunday Market

Half street fair and half sidewalk bazaar, the Taipa Village Sunday market can entertain you for hours. Dozens of street stalls and food stands fill Largo dos Bombeiros and spill down Rua do Regedor to the Pak Tai Temple. *(See map on pg. 101.)* Be sure to check out the village bakeries as well, which are well known for their pastries, Macanese cookies, and nougat candies. Taipa Village is also famous for its wide variety of restaurants, so you will surely eat well when you are done with your shopping. For a particularly authentic Portuguese meal in a small, family-run restaurant, try O Infante on Rua das Virtudes. *(Market open Sunday 11 a.m. to 8 p.m.)*

Coloane Village

Let's be honest—nobody goes to Coloane Village to shop. They go for the traditional village atmosphere and the good eating. That said, many tourists from Taiwan or Hong Kong buy salted fish on Largo do Cais (Dock Square), while plenty of Western visitors buy egg tarts from Lord Stow's Bakery. Chinese and Western tourists alike buy antiques, especially along the appropriately named Rua dos Negociantes (Dealers Street). That said, don't expect to leave Coloane with bulging shopping bags.

The Macau Landmark

The arcade in the five-star Macau Landmark hotel claims to be the most upscale shopping venue in the entire city. This bazaar of international brand names features the likes of Calvin Klein and Hugo Boss, though this indoor mall lacks the panache of similar emporiums in Hong Kong. You could drop a lot of cash here if you wanted to, though you could spend it even more quickly if you went one floor up to the Las Vegas-like Pharaoh's Palace Casino. This Egyptian-themed gambling emporium borders on the hallucinatory, which makes it worth visiting even if you don't gamble. *(Shops open daily 10 a.m. to 9 p.m. See map on pg. 72.)*

New Yaohan Department Store

At the New Yaohan on Avenida da Amizade you can walk the mall, Macau-style. The city's only true megastore, the New Yaohan sells everything from clothing to electronics. The inexpensive food court on the mall's top floor focuses on Asian fare, though you can get Western fast food, too. This can be convenient if you get off the ferry from Hong Kong with an empty stomach, as a skybridge links the New Yaohan to the ferry terminal. *(See map on pg. 72.)* The New Yaohan's symbiotic relationship with the ferry terminal also makes it a good place to spend any leftover pataca at the end of your trip to Macau, especially considering that the duty-free shops in the terminal offer an unimaginative and surprisingly limited array of liquor and perfumes. Sadly, the New Yaohan faces demolition for yet another huge construction project and will have to be relocated. *(Open daily 11 a.m. to 10:30 p.m.)*

Best Buys in Macau

Looking for souvenirs or good deals? Here is my list of the best buys in Macau.

Portuguese Wine, Port, and Brandy

Macau can sometimes seem like a giant liquor store with an extensive wine list priced to undercut any market in Asia, Hong Kong included. You can buy bottles of quite drinkable table wine for as little as MOP$30. The Pavilions Supermercado at 421 Avenida da Praia Grande has a particularly well-stocked wine cellar with a wide variety of prices. *(See map on pg. 153. Open 10:00 a.m. to 9 p.m. Monday to Saturday. Sunday 11 a.m. to 8 p.m.)*

Postage Stamps

Even if you are not a philatelist, you might still consider picking up some Macau commemorative stamp sheets. These works of art are suitable for framing, and best of all, you pay only the face value of the stamps. Stop in at the central post office on the corner of Senate Square, which has a special shop dedicated to stamp collecting.

Antiques

Timeworn goods on sale range from kitschy Chairman Mao watches to beautiful old wooden chests smelling of camphor. With a little bargaining, the price is generally right.

Flowers

Look for flower stands in the alleys around Senate Square or at municipal markets. Prices improve as the day goes on, and by midday MOP$10 will buy you a huge bouquet of fresh flowers.

Museum Ticket Stubs

With entry fees that range from free to MOP$15, the city's excellent museums offer one of the best deals going in Macau.

Chinese and Portuguese Sausage and Pressed Meat

Though not particularly appetizing on first glance, these specialty meats are actually quite tasty. You may have to eat them before you get home, however, as agricultural regulations likely prohibit the importation of meat products to your home country. Prices vary, but a half-pound can be as little as MOP$25.

Chinese Cookies

A real Macau specialty, often flavored with almond, and best enjoyed with Oolong tea. Smaller packages start at MOP$10.

Box of Egg Tarts

Who is kidding whom? You will eat the whole box before you even get off the ferry back to Hong Kong, much less off the plane back home. Some of the best egg tarts can be found at Lord Stow's Bakery in Coloane Village. *(See map on pg. 121.)* In the city, try Margaret's Café

e Nata at 17B Rua do Comandante Mata e Oliveira, which is a short walk from Senate Square, and 41A Rua do Almirante Costa Cabral. *(See maps on pg. 72 and 160.)*

Hell Money

Despite their high denominations, a packet of these bills won't set you back much. They make great bookmarks as well as conversation pieces.

Feng Shui Mirrors

So maybe you don't believe in evil spirits, much less that a mirror mounted above your front door could scare them away from your house. But why not bring one of these shiny little mirrors home just in case?

Joss Sticks

Burn these in the requisite sets of three when you get home, and the smell will instantly transport you back to Macau. Look for joss sticks, *feng shui* mirrors, and hell money in the shops on and around Tercena Street. *(See map on pg. 153.)*

Pataca and Hong Kong Dollars: The Two Currencies of Macau

As any visitor quickly discovers, two completely different currencies circulate in Macau—the Macanese pataca (MOP) and the Hong Kong dollar (HKD). Fortunately, both currencies have roughly the same value, with one pataca more or less equaling one Hong Kong dollar.

The largest banks in Macau and Hong Kong issue the local currency rather than government treasuries, though they do so under strict government oversight. The banks must hold foreign exchange equivalent to the value of the currency they print. Two banks in Macau issue pataca, while three banks in Hong Kong issue Hong Kong dollars. All five banks use different designs on their bills, though they do use the same color for each denomination. All HK$20 notes are blue, for example. All this sounds confusing, but the only thing you really have to pay attention to is the denomination of your bills—it doesn't matter which bank issued your pataca and Hong Kong dollars.

By law, all prices in Macau must be posted in pataca, though you can pay with either pataca or Hong Kong dollars. You can even pay with a mix of both. Generally, you will be given change in the same currency you pay in, though this is not always true. This dual-currency system works out well if you are coming from Hong Kong, as you won't need to change money. You can easily pay for everything in Hong Kong dollars, with the exception of the HK$10 coin, which many businesses refuse to accept for reasons that remain unclear. Obviously, any sort of automated vending machine will require pataca coins, and officially you can only use pataca coins on the buses— though bus drivers don't seem too concerned if you drop Hong Kong coins in the fare box.

Keep in mind that if you plan to do some serious shopping in Macau, you will do slightly better by changing U.S. dollars directly to pataca (as opposed to changing your U.S. dollars into Hong Kong dollars and spending those in Macau). A U.S. dollar fetches about eight pataca, but only about 7.75 Hong Kong dollars—a difference that only becomes significant with larger transactions.

The economic relationship between Hong Kong and Macau has never been one between equals, as evidenced by the fact that while you can freely spend Hong Kong dollars in Macau, you can't spend Macanese pataca in Hong Kong. Make sure you spend your last pataca bills in the ferry terminal's duty-free shops before making your voyage back to Hong Kong. Any left-over pataca coins will make great souvenirs, as they are emblazoned with the city's most famous landmarks.

Facts for the Macau-bound Traveler

If you are heading for Macau, here are the basic travel facts you need to know.

Nearly 19 million people visited Macau in 2005, a number made possible in part by the sheer ease of traveling to Macau. A ferry journey from Hong Kong—the most likely way for readers of this guidebook to reach Macau—is not much more complicated than catching a bus across town. Customs and immigration formalities remain largely just that—formalities. Getting around Macau itself is easy as well, with its small size, safe streets, and abundant taxis and buses. To further simplify your trip to Macau, here is what you need to know.

❖   ❖   ❖

A Note on Telephone Numbers

Keep in mind that Macau telephone numbers are listed below without the city's 853 country code, which is not needed for local calls. However, if you call Macau from Hong Kong or anywhere else in the world, you must add the 853 country code before the number.

Hong Kong telephone numbers are listed below without the 01 area code you must use when calling Hong Kong from Macau. However, if you are calling Hong Kong from anywhere else in the world, you must add Hong Kong's 852 country code instead. If you are calling a Hong Kong number as a local call in Hong Kong, you do not need the 01 or 852 prefix—just dial the unadorned number itself.

Traveling to Macau from Hong Kong and Elsewhere

Like so many foreign visitors, you will probably travel to Macau aboard a ferry from Hong Kong. However, you can also fly into Macau's international airport, walk across the border from mainland China, or arrive by ferry from Guangzhou or Shenzhen. You can even swoop in on a helicopter from Hong Kong.

Ferry from Hong Kong

High-speed ferries operated by Turbojet depart from Hong Kong's Shun Tak Centre (200 Connaught Road, Sheung Wan district of Hong Kong Island; accessible from Sheung Wan MTR subway station, exit D). A less commonly used terminal operated by First Ferry offers competing ferry service to Macau from the China Ferry Terminal (Canton

Road behind the Royal Pacific Hotel and Gateway Tower, Tsimshatsui district of Kowloon). Which terminal works for you depends on where you are staying in Hong Kong, though given that Shun Tak Centre squats directly over an MTR station connected to Hong Kong's web of subway lines, you might as well opt for Turbojet with its more frequent sailings.

Turbojet ferries run 24 hours a day, leaving every 15 minutes during peak hours. The less-frequent First Ferry boats depart every half hour. In both cases the 40-mile (65 km) journey takes about an hour, with one-way ticket costs ranging from MOP$140 to 180 (US$18 to 23). Advance ticket purchases are not generally necessary, except during holidays and weekends, when ferry seats sell out. Sail during a weekday if at all possible.

Make sure that you give yourself enough time to board your ferry. Remember that after buying your ticket you will still have to pass through customs and immigration. This can slow you down, so buying a ticket for a ferry leaving within 30 minutes is pushing things. Sixty minutes is far safer, especially since you must be on board your ferry 15 minutes before its scheduled departure time.

You definitely do not want to miss your ferry, as tickets have zero

flexibility. If you are not on board your ferry when it leaves the dock, then you are out of luck and will have to buy a new ticket. Don't expect a refund on your old ticket either. All this means you should buy a one-way ticket to Macau if you are not sure when you will be returning to Hong Kong.

Officially, both ferry companies require you to check large bags for an additional MOP$20 to 40 fee (US$2.50 to 5), depending on the weight of the bag. However, this policy does not seem to be enforced. If you have a large bag you would rather lug on board yourself, nobody will stop you. In fact, the ferry crew will cheerfully steer you to the luggage racks for oversized bags. On the other hand, if you have large bags, you can always check them and let somebody else do the lugging.

Those prone to seasickness should keep an eye on the weather, as rides are occasionally rough enough to unsettle the stomach. Any ferry trip will be smoother if you sit in the middle of the ship on the lower deck; avoid the bow on a stormy day as you can be literally tossed from your seat if you don't fasten your safety belt.

All ferries have restrooms as well as cafés selling coffee, tea, beer, and other beverages. On many sailings you don't even need to get up, as the café staff will come to your seat and ask what you would like to drink.

Once you arrive in Macau, buses 3 and 3A will take you from the ferry terminal to Senate Square, starting point of all the walks described in chapter four. Other buses depart to various destinations around the city. Ranks of taxis are always waiting outside the terminal as well. *(See "Buses, Taxis, and Trishaws" on pg. 175.)*

For more information, check out Turbojet's website at **www.turbojet.com.hk**. In Hong Kong, call them at 2859-3333 for general enquiries and 2921-6688 for ticketing. In Macau, you can call 790-7039 for general enquiries, though for ticketing you apparently have to call the Hong Kong number. First Ferry's website can be found at **www.nwff.com.hk**. For customer service, call them at 727-676 in Macau and 2131-8181 in Hong Kong.

Helicopter from Hong Kong

If you want to experience a truly amazing ride, take a 16-minute flight from Hong Kong to Macau aboard a sleek HeliExpress S76C helicopter. The heliports are located atop Hong Kong's Shun Tak Centre ferry terminal and the Macau ferry terminal. While the ride costs up to MOP$1,800 (US$225) one-way, you do get the thrill of the ride, which includes spectacular views of the Hong Kong city skyline, the mountainous island of Lantau,

and the busy shipping lanes of the Pearl River Delta. You will also get a bird's eye view of Macau that even beats the 61st floor of the Macau Tower. For more information, see the HeliExpress website at **www.helihongkong.com**. For reservations, dial 2108-9898 in Hong Kong and 727-288 in Macau.

Macau International Airport

If you fly into Macau International—known officially by its airport code of MFM and unofficially by its unfortunate acronym of MIA—you will land at a modern facility that smoothly moves up to 90,000 arriving passengers through its terminal each month. This movement is so smooth, in fact, that the airport boasts you can be in a taxi just 30 minutes after walking off your incoming flight.

That taxi can take you anywhere you want to go in Macau for about MOP$50 (US$6.25). Given Macau's small size, your ride will probably last less than 15 minutes. Alternatively, you could take the bus, which is both slower and cheaper. Bus AP1 runs from the airport to Taipa, continues on to downtown Macau, and ends its route at the border gate (MOP$6 or US$0.75). Bus 21 runs to Coloane Village via Taipa (MOP$4 or US$0.50).

Macau International caters almost exclusively to travelers arriving from mainland Chinese cities or Taipei and Kaoshiung in Taiwan, though there are a limited number of flights to other Asian capital cities. Currently there are no flights to destinations outside East or Southeast Asia, but Air Macau is reported to be negotiating codeshare agreements with international airlines flying to Europe.

An increasing number of low-cost carriers use Macau International, which is a much cheaper airport to operate out of than Hong Kong's Chek Lap Kok International. These budget carriers include Macau Asia Express, Viva Macau, Air Asia, Transasia Airways, and Tiger Airways. If you are flying to destinations in Asia, Macau International may offer cheaper flights than you can get out of Hong Kong's international airport. For a complete flight schedule at Macau International, check out the airport's website at **www.macau-airport.com**.

Air Macau, the city's flagship carrier, offers the most flights in and out of the city. The airline's main office can be found at 398 Alameda Dr. Carlos D'Assumpcao; for ticketing and reservations call 396-5666. In Hong Kong, dial the toll-free 800-966-676.

You can check out the Air Macau website at **www.airmacau.com.mo**.

Travel from/to Mainland China

When residents of Macau want to cross into mainland China, they simply walk across the frontier into Zhuhai at the Portas do Cerco border crossing at the top of the Macau Peninsula. Relatively few foreigners enter China this way, though there is nothing particularly complicated about doing so. If you wish to cross into China here, all you need is the requisite visa in your passport. China Travel Service can arrange for your Chinese visa. Their main office is on Rua de Nagasaki (tel. 700-888). For more information, consult their English-language website at **www.chinatravel1.com/english**. While you can also arrange for your own Chinese visa at the border, this can involve long lines and other hassles—and you will only get a three-day visa good only in the Zhuhai Special Economic Zone that borders Macau.

You can also reach China by ferry. Though most of the ships at the Macau ferry terminal run between Macau and Hong Kong, a smaller number of ferries shuttle passengers between Macau and the mainland Chinese cities of Guangzhou and Shenzhen. Contact Turbojet or First Ferry for more information. *(See "Ferry from Hong Kong" on pg. 175.)*

The Yuet Tung Shipping Company operates out of the little-known pier 14 terminal on Rua das Lorchas. They offer the cheapest ferry service to Shenzhen for MOP$100 (US$12.50). Departure times are 10 a.m., 2 p.m., and 5:30 p.m., though you would be wise to confirm this before heading for the terminal (tel. 574-478). Yuet Tung also runs a ferry across the Inner Harbor to Zhuhai, which costs MOP$12.5 (US$1.50) and takes ten minutes.

If you wish to travel between Macau and Guangzhou by land, Kee Kwan Motor Road Company buses depart frequently between 8 a.m. and 6:30 p.m. You will find one bus stop near the Masters Hotel on the corner of Avenida de Almeida Ribeiro and Rua das Lorchas, but your best bet is to catch the bus after first going through passport control at the border. You can do this by going to floor UG2 of the immigration building after you have been stamped out of Macau. The bus ride costs MOP$55 (US$7), takes about two and a half hours under ideal conditions, and concludes with stops at major hotels in Guangzhou. The company can be reached at 933-888. Currently Kee Kwan's website is Chinese-language only; however, there is always the hope that an English and/or Portuguese version might soon be online (**www.keekwan.com**).

Passports and Entering Macau

Passports and Arrival Cards

To enter Macau you need your passport, since you will be crossing an international border. You will also need to fill out an arrival card, which your ferry crew will distribute before you arrive at the terminal in Macau. Though passport control inside the terminal can sometimes involve long lines, it is otherwise hassle-free if your documents are in order. The immigration police will stamp your passport and take your arrival card, but leave a carbon copy of the card in your passport. Do not lose this carbon copy, as the immigration police will collect it from you upon your departure from Macau.

As befits its long history as an open trading port, Macau has a relaxed attitude towards visas. Citizens of the United States, Canada, Australia, New Zealand, and most European countries are allowed to stay in Macau visa-free for either 30 or 60 days, depending on the country. Hong Kong residents can stay for up to one year. For more information, see the Macau Government Tourist Office's website at **www.macautourism.gov.mo**. The Macau SAR immigration police website can be found at **www.fsm.gov.mo**, but at present only offers Chinese and Portuguese-language webpages.

Customs

You are unlikely to be pulled aside for a customs inspection when entering Macau. In any case, you are allowed to bring in as much cash as you like—no surprise, given Macau's reliance on casino gaming—as well as alcohol and tobacco for personal consumption.

While you are not likely to face a customs inspection upon returning to Hong Kong, the rules there are stricter. You can bring back one liter of alcohol and up to 200 cigarettes or 50 cigars. If you are a Hong Kong resident, however, this limit is reduced to a single bottle of alcohol, 100 cigarettes or 25 cigars. After that, you have to declare your booze and smokes. Fireworks, which are legal in Macau, are illegal in Hong Kong. It goes without saying that narcotics of any sort will get you tossed in the slammer in both Hong Kong and Macau.

Macau Government Tourist Office (MGTO)

In Macau

Picking up a free city map from a MGTO office should be one of your first priorities when you arrive in Macau. In addition to their very useful maps, the MGTO also offers an array of excellent brochures and the services of a cheerful multilingual staff.

The MGTO's main office on Senate Square has been relocated to the oddly named Hot Line building at 335-341 Alameda Dr. Carlos D'Assumpcao in the NAPE district *(see map on pg. 72)*. However, most visitors will find the MGTO branch office in the ferry terminal to be more conveniently located (open daily 9 a.m. to 10 p.m.). Another branch can be found in the airport (open daily 9 a.m. to 6 p.m.). Smaller MGTO offices can be found at the ruins of St. Paul's Church, the Guia Hill lighthouse, and the Portas do Cerco border gate. Hours at these offices generally run from 9 a.m. to 6 p.m., with a siesta break from 1 p.m. to 2 p.m.

You can call the MGTO at 315-566. A separate tourist hotline can be reached at 333-000 and a tourist assistance service at 340-390. The MGTO's website contains a wealth of information as well (**www.macautourism.gov.mo**).

In Hong Kong

In Hong Kong, the MGTO has a conveniently located office in Shun Tak Centre near the ticket counters for the Macau ferries. Stop in and stock up on brochures and maps, which you can read during the hour-long ferry ride (tel. 2857-2287 and open daily 9 a.m. to 1 p.m. and 2:15 to 5:30 p.m.). The MGTO also maintains a counter in the arrivals hall of Hong Kong's Chek Lap Kok International Airport.

Buses, Taxis, and Trishaws

Buses

Macau has an extensive bus system comprising some 360 bus stops and about 40 bus routes. Two different bus companies provide service—Transmac and TCM, which formerly ran ferries to Taipa in the pre-bridge days. Both companies charge identical fares, so from your perspective, it hardly matters which company's bus you end up on. Just get on the first bus heading to your destination.

The bus routes on the Macau peninsula are too extensive to list here. Suffice to say that any major and many minor streets will have at least one bus stop, and that you can determine when/where a bus is going by the schedule posted at the bus stop and the destination sign mounted on the front of the bus. Even if you are not completely sure that you have the right bus, don't be afraid to just jump aboard. After all, Macau is too small for you to go seriously astray, and even if you choose the wrong bus, you're only out MOP$2.5 (US$0.30)—the standard fare for all routes on the Macau peninsula.

If you are heading out to Taipa, you have a half-dozen buses to choose from. Buses 11, 22, 28A, 33, 34, and AP1 all run out to Taipa. Regardless of where you board the bus, you must pay a flat-rate fare of MOP$3.3 (US$0.40).

Buses 21, 21A, 25, and 26A also run to Taipa, but then continue on to Coloane. The fare is MOP$4 (US$0.50) to Coloane Village and MOP$5 (US$0.60) to Hac Sa Beach. Bus 15 runs just between Taipa and Coloane for MOP$2.8 (US$0.35).

Several websites provide detailed information on bus fares and routes, including **www.cityguide.gov.mo**. TCM's English-language website describes all of its bus routes (**www.tcm.com.mo**). Transmac's website, however, appears to be Chinese-language only at this point (**www.transmac.com.mo**).

At present Macau does not have an automated metro pass system like Hong Kong's Octopus card, so if you take the bus be prepared to pay cash. This requires a fistful of pataca coins, as exact change is required for the bus fare. Bus drivers never give change, though they certainly don't mind if you have to overpay as a result. It's unclear if Hong Kong coins are acceptable or not, but if you drop them in the fare box the driver certainly won't kick you off the bus.

❖ ❖ ❖

Taxis

Macau has 750 licensed taxis, according to the Statistics and Census Bureau. All of them have meters and the drivers are generally honest. Don't assume they will speak English, however, and keep in mind that the English and Portuguese names for destinations will be meaningless to a Cantonese-speaking taxi driver. If possible, have your destination written down in Chinese. Black-colored taxis can be flagged down, whereas yellow radio taxis generally have to be called (tel. 939-939, 398-8800, or 519-519).

Supposedly, the maximum fare you could ever pay is MOP$80 (US$10), which would involve a journey all the way from the top of the Macau peninsula to the bottom of Coloane Island. Flag-fall (i.e., the minimum fare) starts at MOP$10 (US$1.25). A MOP$2 (US$0.25) surcharge applies to journeys between Taipa and Coloane; between Macau and Coloane the surcharge increases to MOP$5 (US$0.60). Each bag stored in the trunk will cost you MOP$3 (US$0.35).

Trishaws

Peddle-powered trishaws (pedicabs) still ply their trade in Macau, though they serve more as tourist entertainment than a form of practical transport. The drivers are supposed to have a list of destinations with predetermined fares, so in theory you shouldn't have to haggle over the price of a ride. You can often find a trishaw or two on Senate Square or at the ferry terminal, though a far larger number congregate around the Lisboa Hotel. You will pay around MOP$150 (US$19) for an hour-long tour of the city, but don't expect it to include the steep streets leading up to the Guia Hill lighthouse or the cathedral atop Penha Hill. After all, the trishaw drivers are impressively fit, but they aren't superhuman. If you want to take a photo of a trishaw, ask for permission first and determine whether the driver will make you pay for the privilege.

Moke Jeeps and Rental Cars

Mokes

Nobody seems to rent Mokes anymore, though tourist brochures and websites about Macau would lead you to believe the streets of the city are clogged with these odd miniaturized jeeps. I don't think I've ever seen one on the road myself, which I hardly find surprising. After all, these open-sided jeeps lack air-conditioning and scream out "tourist" like a neon sign. I don't recommend renting a Moke, unless you like being the smallest, slowest, and oldest vehicle on the road. Mokes are so old, in fact, that the last of them will be retired in 2007 when they come up against new regulations prohibiting commercial rental of vehicles over ten years old. If you can't resist the lure of these pint-size jeeps in the meantime, Avis will happily rent you one of its 14 Mokes. You can forget about renting from the archrival Happy Mokes, as they have already shut down as a result of the ten-year rule. Keep in mind that Mokes always have stick shifts, so if you don't know how to drive with a standard transmission, you can't operate one of these glorified go-carts.

Rental Cars

I don't recommend renting a full-sized car either, for the simple reason that Macau is very small and endowed with plenty of taxis and buses. A rental car just isn't necessary, unless you need the car for some special purpose like hauling around a video film crew—and even then you would be better served by renting a car *and* a driver. In this case, you have to go to Avis, the only rental car firm in the city. You can find Avis on the ground floor of the ferry terminal (tel. 726-571 and open daily 10 a.m. to 1 p.m. and 2 p.m. to 4 p.m.) as well as in the car park of the Mandarin Oriental on Avenida da Amizade (tel. 336-789 and open daily 8 a.m. to 7 p.m.). You can make reservations in advance of your arrival on their website at **www.avis.com.mo**. Most of their rental cars come with automatic transmissions.

Driver's Licenses

According to Avis, citizens of the United States, Portugal, Hong Kong, Australia, New Zealand, the United Kingdom, and a few other somewhat random countries including obscure Sao Tome e Principe can drive with their own national driver's license, though they will still have to register with the Macau Traffic Department. Canadians—and citizens of most other countries—apparently need an international driver's license, but check with Avis, as the rules may change. Regardless of your citizenship, you will certainly need some strong nerves to drive Macau's narrow streets, which can sometimes seem like giant video games full of zigzagging motor-scooters and careening buses. You will also need to have a credit card and be at least 21 years of age.

Drive on the Left

When driving in Macau you must keep to the left, as in Great Britain. This is yet another example of how Hong Kong has influenced Macau. Automotively speaking, Macau took its cue from British-ruled Hong Kong, which drives on the left—even though in both mainland China and Portugal everyone drives on the right.

Languages

Cantonese and Portuguese are the official languages of Macau. More than 95% of the population speaks Cantonese as their first language, making it the lingua franca of the city. A relatively small number of people speak Portuguese, though the colonial tongue remains highly visible. Government documents and websites are always produced in both Portuguese and Cantonese, for example, and street names and traffic signs are posted in both languages. Since Macau's return to China in 1999, an increasing number of people in Macau have learned Mandarin (also known as Putonghua), the dominant language of mainland China. These days most Cantonese learning a European language choose English over Portuguese, and many Macau residents speak at least some English. While you should not expect everyone in Macau to speak English, you can safely assume that you will find staff who speak English at any hotel, restaurant, shop, or public institution that routinely deals with foreigners.

❖ ❖ ❖

Newspapers, Books, and Maps

You can get free city maps at the Macau Government Tourist Office branches in the ferry terminal and airport. Most visitors will find that these maps are detailed enough for their needs. However, you should buy *Atlas de Macau* (MOP$110 or US$14) if you need more detailed cartographic resources for finding your way around the city. The maps in this hardcover book cover all of Macau and have a much greater level of detail than the free MGTO maps. If you need maps with an even higher level of detail, I recommend the excellent *Arruamentos da Regiao Administrativa Especial de Macau* (a bargain at MOP$30 or US$4). The maps in this book work best for research purposes rather than actually navigating city streets. Both books feature bilingual Portuguese and Chinese-language text.

For books and maps on Macau, your best bet is the Portuguese Bookshop (Livraria Portuguesa e Galeria de Art) at 18–20 Rua de Sao Domingos, just off Senate Square. *(See map on pg. 153.)* As its name suggests, the shop focuses on Portuguese-language books; however, it stocks a limited number of English-language books. If you want books and maps on Macau, this is likely your best bet. (Open

Monday to Saturday 10 a.m. to 8 p.m. and Sunday 12 p.m. to 7 p.m.) Other possibilities include the giftshop of the Macau Museum *(see pg. 56)*.

Hong Kong's *South China Morning Post* serves as Macau's main English-language newspaper, though it rarely contains much news on the city. The *Macau Post* is a daily newspaper with local news, but it tends to focus on news related to the gaming industry. The same is true of the monthly magazine *Macau Business*. The newsstand under the arcades on Senate Square is a convenient place to pick up copies of all three publications.

Hotels and Pousadas

Like most visitors to Macau, you are probably not planning to stay overnight. Should you opt to spend the night, however, the city has a large number of hotel rooms. Prices climb and vacancies plummet during weekends, so plan to stay during the week if possible.

For a true Macanese experience, I recommend staying at a pousada (the Portuguese word for "a place of blessed repose," though it is often translated as the more prosaic "inn"). If you want to stay in a hotel with authentic Macanese atmosphere, for example, book a room at the luxurious Pousada de Sao Tiago. *(See pg. 64.)* For a more affordable option, consider the Pousada de Mong-Ha. This hilltop inn is part of the government-run Institute for Tourism Studies that trains future workers for the hospitality industry. If you wish to stay out on quiet Coloane Island, consider the family-run Pousada de Coloane, with its beach and ocean view. For a romantic getaway, this might be your best bet. All three pousadas have well-regarded restaurants serving a blend of Portuguese, Macanese, and international dishes.

Pousada de Sao Tiago
Avenida da Republica
Twin rates start at MOP$2,600 (US$325), with suites going for as much as MOP$6,000 (US$750).
Tel. 378-111
www.saotiago.com.mo
(See map on pg. 63.)

Pousada de Coloane
Cheoc Van Beach, Coloane
Twin rates start at MOP$750 (US$94)
Tel. 882-143
www.hotelpcoloane.com.mo
(See map on pg. 134.)

Pousada de Mong-Ha
Rampa do Forte de Mong Ha
Twin rates start at MOP$600 (US$75) on weekdays and rise to MOP$800 (US$100) on weekends.
Tel. 555-222
www.ift.edu.mo
(See map on pg. 160.)

Keep in mind that despite its name, the Pousada Marina Infante is a regular hotel and most definitely not a pousada.

In addition to the pousadas, Macau offers a wide selection of hotels, some of which are luxurious but few of which have much character. Alternatively, the city has quite a few cheaper hotels of varying quality.

I have listed the city's major hotels below. Nearly all have websites, so you can have a look at what these hotels have to offer before making a decision about where you want to stay. Keep in mind that you generally will not get the best room rate when you book through a hotel website. I have found that hotel booking sites like **www.directrooms.com** can usually beat the room rates available through a hotel's own website, sometimes by a significant amount. Another tactic is to book a room through one of the travel agents found in the Shun Tak Centre in Hong Kong, near the Macau ferry ticket counters. More of these agents can be found in the terminal in Macau as well.

The following upmarket hotels generally have a rack rate of more than US$200. (The rack rate is the undiscounted price you would pay if you walked into a hotel and spent the night without prior reservations.) However, during certain times of year you will likely be able to book discounted room rates.

Landmark Hotel
555 Avenida da Amizade
Tel. 781-781
www.landmarkhotel.com.mo
(See map on pg. 72.)

Lisboa Hotel
2-4 Avenida de Lisboa
Tel. 377-666
www.hotelisboa.com
(See map on pg. 72.)

Mandarin Oriental
Avenida da Amizade
Tel. 567-888
www.mandarinoriental.com
(See map on pg. 72.)

Westin Resort Macau
1918 Estrada de Hac Sa, Coloane Tel. 871-111
www.westin-macau.com
(See map on pg. 134.)

The following hotels generally have a rack rate somewhere between US$100 to 200, with discounts sometimes taking you below US$100.

Beverly Plaza
70 Avenida do Dr. Rodrigo Rodrigues
Tel. 782-288
www.beverlyplaza.com

Casa Real (formerly the Nam Yue)
1118 Avenida do Dr. Rodrigo Rodrigues
Tel. 726-288

Emperor Hotel
51 Rua de Xangai
Tel. 781-888
www.emperorhotel.com.mo

Fortuna Hotel
63 Rua de Cantao
Tel. 786-333
www.hotelfortuna.com.mo

Galaxy Waldo
Avenida da Amizade
Tel. 886-688
www.galaxyresorts.com

Golden Crown China Hotel
Macau International Airport
Tel. 851-166
www.htlchina.com.mo

Grandeur Hotel
199 Rua de Pequim
Tel. 781-233
www.hotelgrandeur.com

Grandview Hotel
142 Estrada Governador Albano de Oliveira, Taipa
Tel. 837-788
www.grandview-hotel.com

Guia Hotel
1-5 Estrada do Engenheiro Trigo
Tel. 513-888
www.hotelguia-macau.com

Holiday Inn
82-86 Rua de Pequim
Tel. 783-333
www.macau.holiday-inn.com

New Century Hotel
889 Avenida Padre Tomas Pereira, Taipa   Tel. 831-111
www.newcenturyhotel-macau.net

Pousada Marina Infante
Avenida Olimpica, Taipa
Tel. 838-333
www.pousadamarinainfante.com

Ritz Hotel
7-13 Rua do Comendador Kou Ho Neng
Tel. 339-955
www.ritzhotel.com.mo

Royal Hotel
2-4 Estrada da Vitoria
Tel. 552-222
www.hotelroyal.com.mo

Sintra Hotel
58-62 Avenida de D. Joao IV
Tel. 710-111
www.hotelsintra.com

The following hotels generally have a rack rate below US$100, though rates will rise during peak periods.

Fu Wa Hotel
98-102 Rua de Francisco Xavier Pereira
Tel. 553-838

Kingsway Hotel
230 Rua de Luis Gonzaga Gomes
Tel. 702-888
www.hotelkingsway.com.mo

Macau Masters Hotel
162-178 Rua das Lorchas
Tel. 937-572
www.mastershotel-macau.com

Metropole Hotel
63 Avenida da Praia Grande
Tel. 388-166

Mondial Hotel
8-10 Rua de Antonio Basto
Tel. 566-866

HOTELS IN MACAU

Presidente Hotel
355 Avenida da Amizade
Tel. 553-888
www.hotelpresident.com.mo

Sun Sun
14-16 Praca de Ponte e Horta
Tel. 939-393
www.bestwestern.com

Taipa Hotel
822 Estrada Governador Nobre
Carvalho, Taipa
Tel. 781-233
www.hoteltaipa.com

Budget hotels (rack rate of US$50 or less) generally can't be booked online and almost never have websites or email addresses. An exception is Augusters Lodge, a three-room hostel located close to Senate Square. Dormitory bunks go for MOP$80 (US$10) and rooms go for MOP$150 to 180 (US$19 to 23).

**Augusters Lodge
(formerly Sweet House)**
24 Rua do Dr. Pedro Jose Lobo
Tel. 664-5026 or 713-242
www.sweet-house.de

For an up-to-date listing of budget hotels with addresses and phone numbers, pick up the *Budget Accommodations* brochure from the MGTO office in the ferry terminal when you arrive. Better yet, pick it up at the MGTO branch office in Hong Kong *(see "Macau Government Tourist Office" on pg. 174)* and phone ahead for reservations. Keep in mind that the further down the price range you go, the more likely you are to wind up in a seedy hotel with its own resident band of prostitutes.

Telephone Calls, Email, and Postcards

The cheapest option for local and international phone calls is to buy a CTM (Companhia de Telecomunicacoes de Macau) phone card at a convenience store or similar small shop. Cards can be bought for MOP$50, 100, and 150 (US$6, 12, and 18).

If you own a GSM-standard mobile phone (the kind used everywhere except North America), you can buy a rechargeable CTM SIM card for about MOP$100 (US$12) and presto—you have your own telephone number in Macau. For details, see CTM's website at **www.ctm.net**.

Though courtesy phones are nowhere near as common as in Hong Kong, where you can find them everywhere, large hotels in Macau generally have courtesy phones in their lobbies.

If you are calling home, keep in mind that Macau is eight hours ahead of Greenwich Mean Time. If it's Monday, 11 a.m. in Macau, for example, it's Sunday, 11 p.m. on the East Coast of the United States.

If you need to check your email in Macau—or send me an email telling me how useful this guidebook has/has not been—you have somewhat limited options. For free internet access, you can go to the CTM Mobile Zone shop on either 14H Rua da Barca or 22 Rua de Sao Domingos. The latter location is near Senate Square; you will find the internet terminals on the second floor of the shop. Be prepared to wait for an open terminal. The UNESCO Center on Alameda Dr. Carlos D'Assumpcao offers internet access for a very reasonable MOP$10 (US$1.25) per hour, complete with free cup of coffee (open daily 2 p.m. to 8 p.m.). For more upmarket surroundings, you can try the Cyber Café Verandah in the Landmark Hotel on Avenida da Amizade for MOP$25 (US$3) an hour (open daily 10 a.m. to 10 p.m.).

You can mail your postcards from the main post office on Senate Square, open 9 a.m. to 6 p.m. weekdays and 9 a.m. to 1 p.m. on Saturdays. Branch offices with similar hours can be found throughout Macau, including in the airport and ferry terminal. Alternatively, look for the red postal kiosks stationed throughout the city in strategic locations, which feature mailboxes and coin-operated stamp vending machines.

Health Matters

Fortunately, a journey to Macau requires no special health precautions. No specific immunizations are required and there is no risk of malaria. However, you should protect yourself with the basic immunizations that every traveler should get when they venture abroad, regardless of destination. Consult the Centers for Disease Control's east Asia travel webpage for more information at **www.cdc.gov/travel/eastasia.htm**.

In theory, Macau's tap water is safe to drink. However, the locals don't really trust their tap water and either boil it or rely on jugs of purified water. You may find that gulping down glasses of tap water can lead to an upset stomach, though probably nothing worse. High salinity remains the most common problem with the water, though this is a matter of taste rather than public health. Given all this, you might as well stick to bottled water. Fortunately, a 1.5 liter bottle of Vita-brand water sells for only about MOP$6 (US$0.75).

Take care with the sun during the summer months. Use sunblock and wear a hat and light-colored clothing if you will be in direct sunlight. Keep in mind that a lightweight pair of pants or long skirt is cooler in the direct sun than shorts. Do like the local women and carry an umbrella to ward off the sun—not to mention those torrential summer downpours. Drink as much water as possible and plan your day so that you are outside during the cooler early morning and early evening hours, but are inside during the hottest hours—the air-conditioned Macau Museum is a good place to spend the middle of a summer's day, for example.

If you suffer from a respiratory ailment, be advised that Macau can be shrouded in a somewhat surreal haze of dust and smog during the winter months.

Emergencies

In the event of an emergency requiring the police, fire department, or ambulance service, dial 999 from any telephone. For less urgent situations, you can call the emergency hotline for tourists by dialing 112 from any telephone. For non-emergency police matters, dial 573-333.

Macau has two hospitals capable of handling most medical emergencies. The Conde S. Januario Hospital is on Estrada do Visconde de S. Januario (tel. 313-731) and the Kiang Wu Hospital is on Estrada do Repouso (tel. 371-333). For non-emergency health care, visit one of the city's health clinics. Perhaps the most convenient of these is the Tap Seac Health Centre (Macau Oriental Health Center) located between Rua do Campo and Avenida do Conselheiro

Ferreira de Almeida (tel. 522-232).

Most countries let their Hong Kong consulates handle Macau-related business, with the exception of Portugal, which maintains a consulate at 45 Rua de Pedro Nolasco da Silva (tel. 356-660). So unless you are a Portuguese citizen, you will have to call your consulate in Hong Kong for assistance with lost passports and similar matters. Key telephone numbers for consulates in Hong Kong: Australia (2827-8881); Canada (2810-4321); New Zealand (2877-4488); South Africa (2577-3279); UK (2901-3000); USA (2523-9011). Ireland does not have a consulate, but its honorary consul's office can be reached at 2527-4897 or 2826-8063. A complete listing of contact information for all consulates in Hong Kong can be found at **www.info.gov.hk/protocol/**.

Be sure to carry photocopies of your passport and other key documents with you while traveling, but keep them separate from the original documents. Also, you should write down the emergency customer service numbers on your credit cards and keep them separate from the cards—that way, if the cards are lost or stolen, you can immediately call and cancel them. If you don't have the numbers, you will lose precious time looking them up.

Handicapped Access

Unfortunately, Macau will present many barriers to disabled travelers. Buses are not equipped with wheelchair lifts and the city's historic sites and other older buildings generally do not offer handicapped access of any kind. However, new buildings are often designed to allow handicapped access. At the very least, they will have elevators. Newer hotels often have specially designed rooms for disabled guests; consult hotel websites for more information.

While the ferry terminals and the ferries themselves make no special attempt to cater to disabled travelers, they nonetheless present no insurmountable barriers. The ferry crews can assist handicapped travelers during the boarding process, though don't expect them to be well trained in this sort of duty.

Most curbs do not have sloped ramps for crossing streets and, unlike in Hong Kong, crosswalks are not modified for the blind with audible timers. In many parts of Macau—especially around the ruins of St. Paul's Church—the streets are steep and paved with rough cobbles. However, Senate Square is smoothly paved with tiles and is pedestrian-only. Trails on Taipa and Coloane are primarily gravel or hard-packed dirt, and sometimes contain long flights of steps.

Some good resources for disabled travelers include Access-Able Travel Source (**www.access-able.com**), the travel section of Disabled Online (**www.disabledonline.com**) and Global Access Disabled Travel Network (**www.globalaccessnews.com**).

Money Matters

Cash

Macau is one of the smallest entities in the world to maintain its own currency, which is known as the pataca (MOP). However, the Hong Kong dollar (HKD) is the de-facto second currency of Macau. *(See "The Two Currencies of Macau" on pg. 166.)* Both currencies are roughly equal in value to each other (i.e., one pataca equals one Hong Kong dollar) and share a similar exchange rate to the U.S. dollar—about 8 pataca or 7.75 Hong Kong dollars per U.S. dollar. One Hong Kong dollar equals 100 cents, and one Macanese pataca equals 100 avos.

If you change money in Macau, ask for Hong Kong dollars rather than pataca. This way if you end up with any extra cash at the end of your trip to Macau, you can either spend it back in Hong Kong or simply exchange it for U.S. dollars or other hard currency. You most definitely do *not* want to be stuck with any left-over pataca, however, as you can't spend them outside Macau and you can't change them into any other currency.

You can get your Hong Kong dollars at the currency exchange counters located in the ferry terminal and at the airport. You won't be surprised to find that casinos offer 24-hour currency exchange as well. You can also withdraw Hong Kong dollars or pataca from ATM machines in Macau. ATM machines are linked to the main worldwide systems like Plus and Cirrus. If your ATM card does not work in one ATM, try another machine from a different bank and you might have better luck. Hotel front desks can usually change money as well, though the rates are generally poor.

Traveler's Checks

If you have traveler's checks, you will probably have to change these at a bank. This means planning carefully, as like banks everywhere, those in Macau stick to normal business hours—generally 9 a.m. to 5 p.m. weekdays and 9 a.m. to 1 p.m. on Saturdays. Unlike with cash, you will need your passport when changing traveler's checks.

Credit Cards

Credit cards are widely accepted, though be cautious where you use them. Remember that every time you use your credit card you are sharing your name and credit card information with an unknown number of people with an unknown degree of honesty.

You should also keep in mind that credit card companies monitor transactions for suspicious activity, particularly in high-fraud areas like Hong Kong and Macau, and will limit maximum purchase amounts or simply freeze a card outright if they detect anything that looks shady. If you try to make a large-ticket purchase, for example, you may find that your card won't work, though clever merchants know they can sometimes get around this by breaking the purchase into two separate transactions. Regardless of the transaction amounts, however, making a large number of purchases in quick succession can also cause your card to stop working. In this case your credit card company will have frozen your card as a protective measure until you call to confirm that all is well. You can reduce the chances of this happening by letting your credit card company know in advance when and where you will be traveling overseas.

To Tip or Not to Tip?

In general, Macau conforms to Asian norms when it comes to tipping. Tipping at a restaurant is generally not necessary, as a 10% service charge will be added to the bill. Bellhops should be tipped, with 10 pataca/Hong Kong dollars (about US$1) the suggested rate per bag. Doormen who flag your taxi or perform similar tasks should generally be tipped as well. Tip guides and their drivers at your discretion. You can also tip hairdressers and washroom attendants if you are so inclined; the rate for the former is highly variable, but for the latter one or two pataca will do the trick. You do not need to tip taxi drivers, though rounding up is common—for example, paying MOP$20 for an 18-pataca fare. You do not need to tip coffee baristas either, though the Starbucks on Senate Square does have a prominently displayed tip jar.

Weather

If you can, visit Macau between October and December. At this time of year temperatures hover in the 60s and 70s (15–25C), with low humidity and little rain. If you don't mind chilly temperatures, January through March is not a bad time to visit either. Temperatures average 60 degrees (15C), though lows regularly dip into the 50s (10C) or even upper 40s (7–15C). Plunges into the 30s (-1 to 4C) are possible, but relatively rare. If you come from the snowbelts of Northern Europe and North America, Macau's winters will seem quite tame. In fact, the only snow you will ever see is the artificial stuff on Christmas decorations. Rain is infrequent from October through January, but by February the number of rain days begins to increase.

The summer months of April to September feature high heat and heavy rain. Average daily highs are in the 80s (26–32C), though Macau suffers through plenty of days in the 90s (32–37C). The humidity further exacerbates the heat, as does Macau's urban environment. Rain falls frequently during the summer, with June the wettest month. Heavy summer downpours can leave you drenched no matter how big your umbrella or how extensive your raingear.

Typhoons can strike Macau anywhere between May and November, with August and September the peak months. *(See "Typhoon!" on pg. 91 for more information on these monster storms.)*

In recent years smog has become a weather condition in its own right. Though a problem year round, during the winter months an orangey-brown haze of pollutants can smother Macau in smog thick enough to shut down Macau's international airport. Locals say that the only truly clear days follow big holidays in China, when the factories shut down and the smog blows out to sea. The locals seem to be right—the clearest visibility I have ever seen in the Pearl River Delta occurred the day after New Year's Day.

To keep track of the weather in Macau, all you have to do is dial 1311. Press extension 4 and you will get an English-language weather

WEATHER

WEATHER

report from the Macau Meteorological and Geophysical Bureau, complete with typhoon warnings. This weather service also includes an air-quality report. Alternatively, visit the bureau's website at **www.smg.gov.mo**. The

South China Morning Post, the Hong Kong newspaper that serves as Macau's de-facto English-language paper, also provides detailed daily weather reports.

❖ ❖ ❖

The colonial-era Pharmacia Popular on Senate Square dispenses everything from painkillers to penicillin.

MACAU IN ASIA

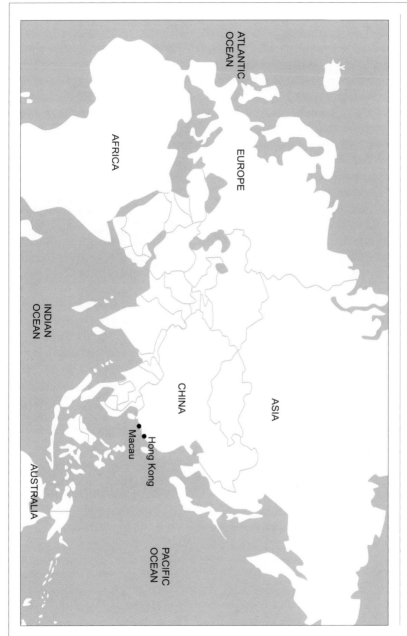

ATLANTIC
OCEAN

AFRICA

EUROPE

INDIAN
OCEAN

CHINA

ASIA

Macau

Hong Kong

AUSTRALIA

PACIFIC
OCEAN

Steven K. Bailey

Steven K. Bailey has written for a variety of travel publications and is a long-time contributor to www.thingsasian.com, a leading website devoted to travel in Asia. He specializes in northern Vietnam, Hong Kong, and Macau. Bailey is currently working on a guidebook to Hong Kong for ThingsAsian Press, due out in 2007. He welcomes email from readers at sbailey@thingsasian.com.

Jill C. Witt

Macau and Hong Kong are some of Jill C. Witt's favorite places to take photos. She also enjoys nature and low-light photography. Her favorite things about Macau: fresh flowers and egg tarts.

Lead Photo Captions

Cover: Giant incense coils do a slow burn at the Hong Kung Temple.

Introduction (pg. 4): Joss sticks burn at the Kun Iam Temple on Taipa Island.

Chapter 1 (pg. 10): Cannons still line the battlements of the Monte Fort.

Chapter 2 (pg. 36): The Macau-bound jetfoil *Taipa* passes small boats near Hong Kong's Cheung Chau Island.

Chapter 3 (pg. 42): The mosaic tiles of Senate Square evoke the sea and Macau's maritime history.

Chapter 4 (pg. 50): Colonial-era buildings line St. Augustine's Square.

Chapter 5 (pg. 86): A barge passes beneath the new Sai Van Bridge.

Chapter 6 (pg. 94): Flowers line the verandah of the Taipa House Museum.

Chapter 7 (pg. 116): Joss sticks smoke outside the Tam Kong Temple in Coloane Village.

Chapter 8 (pg. 140): Food vendors near Rua da Felicidade dish up cheap eats for a hungry late-night crowd.

Chapter 9 (pg. 150): Shoppers browse near St. Dominic's Church.

Chapter 10 (pg. 168): A rickshaw driver pedals his way down the Praia Grande.

Map Legend

◗ = Starting Point ᵼᵼ = Restaurant 🚌 = Bus Stop

P = Parking 🛉 = Restroom ℂ = Telephone ⟋ = Trail

A Transmac bus carries passengers along the Praia Grande.